"YOU'RE GROUNDED TILL YOU'RE THIRTY!"

Good Housekeeping
Parent Guide

"YOU'RE GROUNDED TILL YOU'RE THIRTY!"

What works–and what doesn't–
in parenting today's teens

JUDI CRAIG, PH.D.

HEARST BOOKS
NEW YORK

Library of Congress Cataloging-in Publication Data
Craig, Judith E., 1940-
      "You're grounded till you're thirty!": what works—and what doesn't—
      in parenting today's teens / by Judi Craig.
         p. cm.
      Includes bibliographical references and index.
      ISBN 1-58816-072-6 (formerly 0-688-13196-4)
      1. Parent and teenager—Popular works. 2. Adolescent psychology—
      Popular works. 3. Adolescence—Popular works. I. Title.
      HQ799.15.C7   1996
      649'.125—dc20   95-33480
                                               CIP

This book is not intended as a substitute for the help and services of a trained professional. The reader should regularly consult qualified professionals in matters relating to a child's mental or physical health and particularly to any symptoms or problems that may require diagnosis or other professional attention.

A Skylight Press Book

Printed in the United States of America
5 6 7 8 9 10

Book Design by Lisa Stokes
Cover Design by Remo Cosentino, Bookgraphics

To Sean, Tim, and Lisanne

post-teen survivors who bring great joy—
and never dull moments!

SPECIAL THANKS TO . . .

• Larry Smith, Jr., Ph.D. and Diplomate in Clinical Psychology—psychotherapist *par excellence*, mentor, officemate, and loyal friend of twenty-something years—for his valuable critique of the manuscript, his exuberance for life, and for putting up with all those practical jokes.

• Harry Croft, M.D., Fellow of the American Psychiatric Association and Certified in Addiction Medicine—for his helpful suggestions on the alcohol/drug abuse chapter, for his friendship, and for being a person whose brain I can always pick five minutes before an interview.

• Meg Schneider and Lynn Sonberg of Skylight Press—for their right-on suggestions, fresh insights, and tremendous support throughout all our writing ventures.

• Toni Sciarra, Senior Editor at William Morrow—for getting rid of the blips, typos, and split infinitives, for putting on all the right polishing touches, and for her ready availability and encouragement.

Contents

PART I
SOME BASICS

O N E

WHAT'S REALLY GOING ON WITH YOUR TEEN?

I f there's one thought that's likely to raise a parent's anxiety about his or her young child, it's *Just wait until he gets to be a teenager!* And once that eventful day actually dawns, few parents can ignore it. The entry of a youngster into the world of adolescence is usually heralded loudly and clearly by a dramatic and often disconcerting struggle for independence.

This independence involves a teenager's learning to become comfortable with an adult body, to use good judgment in making decisions, and to relate well to peers of both sexes; it also involves her grappling with emerging sexuality, making tentative educational and work/career choices, and preparing to support herself financially. In other words, adolescence is a time when a person begins to form a full identity, a belief about who she is: her capabilities and weaknesses, her preferences, her sexuality, her emerging values and philosophy, and her hopes and dreams.

Obviously, this complicated process does not happen peacefully. It's a tumultuous process for the teen, fraught with insecurity, ambivalence, frustration, confusion, and anxiety. With mood changes that can range from enthusiastic excitement to utter despair, is it any wonder that an adolescent can act with impressive maturity one minute and then behave like a two-year-old the next?

Understandably, parents are somewhat apprehensive as the child they have known begins to enter this intense time of change. They realize that they can be in for some real battles as their teen questions, confronts, disagrees with, and tests them. They know that their advice, opinions, and values are likely to be challenged as he switches his loyalties to his peer group. They think of all the potential dangers he can face as he spends more free time away from the protection of home, especially once he and his friends are able to drive. They begin to worry more about things like drugs, alcohol, sex, pregnancy, and gangs. Most of all, they feel anxious about the knowledge that they will have less control over their teen's environment, personal choices, and behavior with each passing year. The end result is that parents of adolescents can find themselves by turns confused, irritated, frightened, hurt, enraged, and/or overwhelmed.

To better prepare yourself for this new phase in your child's development (and in your own!), this book will help you understand what is going on in the body, mind, and heart of a teenager. It will help you talk to your teen in such a way that he'll be more likely to open up and to listen to you. It will help you set reasonable guidelines and rules, decreasing the chance for power struggles between the two of you. Most important, it will enable you to navigate through many specific and troublesome moments with confidence—whether it's a teen who challenges your house rules, or rolls her eyes when you talk, or announces that she's in love with someone you consider less than wonderful—and still end up with a good relationship with your offspring.

YOUNGER TEEN VERSUS OLDER TEEN

The word *teenager* represents a seven-year time span. Since children mature at different rates, it's difficult to make generalizations about any specific age group. Nevertheless, it's obvious that the concerns and problems of younger adolescents can be quite different from those of older ones. For our purposes, we'll arbitrarily define younger teens as thirteen- through fifteen-year-olds and older teens as sixteen- through nineteen-year-olds.

Younger teens are grappling with newly changing bodies as puberty rushes in full-force. This makes them highly self-conscious about their appearance and accounts for those lingering looks in the mirror for which adolescents are so well known.

It's at this time that the telephone becomes an issue in many households, as younger teens begin that loyalty switch from parents to peer group. Emotionally and financially, young adolescents typically remain quite dependent on their parents, a fact that in most cases presses them even more to prove that they can handle things just fine without adult intervention. Mood swings are common, with younger teens vacillating between a *Let me do it* my *way!* stance and bewildered thoughts of *What should I do now*? Parents, of course, find it frustrating or even infuriating as younger teens insist that they don't want to be treated "like babies" and then turn around and behave with childlike immaturity.

Older teens have had some time to adjust to their new bodies and are usually beginning the process of coming to terms with the positives and negatives that they see reflected in the mirror. They typically have a clearer sense of their sexuality and have begun to date.

Most late teens have become far less dependent on their parents both physically and emotionally. They typically have a great deal of mobility (especially if they drive) and are likely to spend little time at home. They push hard to come and go as they please and spend much more of their time unsupervised by adults.

Older teens are increasingly aware that the day they will leave home is fast approaching, and many are beginning to struggle with decisions about education and career plans. Many, for better or worse, are involved in a serious romantic relationship or may be agonizing over the fact that they are not yet involved in one. Many are employed part-time and may even be taking over some or all of their own financial support.

COMMON STRUGGLES

To give you a clearer perspective on normal adolescent development, let's look at the common issues confronting today's teens. By understanding them, you'll be better prepared to take appropriate action to protect your teenager when necessary while still honoring her needs and feelings.

A DIFFERENT BODY

Although most adults think of puberty as a hallmark of adolescence, many youngsters (especially girls) have long since passed puberty by the time they become teenagers. However, the bulk of teens still face these significant body changes in the thirteen- to fourteen-year age range (and a few will not experience these changes until the age of sixteen). Teens have growth spurts, their reproductive systems develop and begin functioning, and their bodies grow hair in new places. Their hormones begin to surge, and they become sexual beings.

With all these physical changes, almost all adolescents worry about their appearance. They'll scrutinize every inch of their bodies for evidence that they measure up to whatever they think the current standard of okayness is. While the rest of the world might see a teen's body as enviably perfect, the teen herself might fret about the most minute aspect of its proportions. Basic aspects of anatomical structure such as height, bone structure, nose shape, chest size, and genitals become obvious targets for concern. So do hair and pimples.

Nor do adolescents escape our culture's preoccupation with thinness. Since body weight is an important factor in a person's self-esteem, teens who are overweight (or who think they are) can suffer immensely. Teen girls, in particular, are known for believing that they are "fat" when in fact they aren't. Both sexes have the expectation that they *should* look like the popular teenage television and movie stars, so teens who don't are likely seriously to question their attractiveness.

EARLY AND LATE BLOOMERS

As if adolescence doesn't bring enough trials and tribulations of its own, there are two special groups for which things can be even more difficult: early and late bloomers. The early bloomer enters puberty during the preteen years, developing an adult body while the majority of the youngster's peers still look like children.

Boys who are early bloomers are usually admired by their same-age peers. They are bigger and taller and, if they're athletically inclined, they might shine in sports. Because of their size and physical maturity, however, they often have the burden of inappropriate expectations placed on them by their parents and teachers. Adults just expect them to act older and to have more emotional maturity than should be expected of preteens.

Girls who are early bloomers are often ridiculed by their peers and feel terribly awkward and embarrassed by the obvious signs of their sexual maturity. They are especially vulnerable if they are large-breasted, as they are often eyed with not-so-subtle curiosity by the boys. Unfortunately, there is also the inaccurate but common perception among their peers that big-chested girls are engaging in sexual activity. Some early-developing girls will go to great lengths to disguise the fact that they have breasts, even wearing sweaters or jackets indoors when the temperature is warm.

Other early-blooming girls seem to be envied and admired by their peers. Unfortunately, they may begin to flaunt their emerging sexuality and often become vulnerable to getting involved with boys beyond their level of maturity. Unless held in check by a parent, they will dress provocatively and wear inappropriate makeup. Many become flirtatious with older boys and even adult men. It is as if they are using their newly developed bodies as a means of getting all the attention they can.

The boy who is a late bloomer is likely to feel like he's in a time warp. He fears the ridicule of other boys, especially in the locker room. He's likely to be as yet unconcerned about girls and sex, so what can he talk about with his male buddies? His peers treat him like he's everyone's little brother, at best; like some kind of mutant, at worst. No matter how many times his doctor or his parents reassure him that he will mature eventually, he still wonders if something awful is wrong with him.

When a girl matures later than the majority of her peers, (perhaps not until she's sixteen), she questions whether or not she will ever be a "real woman." She's especially likely to worry about her ability to have children, and she prays for the day she'll begin menstruating as validation of her true femininity. While she's probably more emotionally mature than her late-blooming male counterpart, she is still likely to be emotionally and socially out of sync with her peers. Consequently, she often remains on the social sidelines, especially where the opposite sex is concerned, remaining an adolescent in limbo.

BECOMING INDEPENDENT

To be emotionally independent is to be able to make one's own choices. This means that no matter how much you love or respect someone, you might choose to do something that does not meet with that person's approval.

A young person cannot become emotionally independent without going through a questioning process. If she accepts what she is told by her parents, teachers, religious leaders, peers, and the representatives of society's institutions without first examining their messages, she'll either become a rigid thinker who sees anyone who disagrees with her as wrong or she'll be vulnerable to being led in any direction by the popular ideas of the times. Either result leads to a person who stops growing emotionally and spiritually.

It's important to realize that a little rebellion on the part of your teenager is healthy. If she agrees with everything you tell her, she's not going through that questioning process that is so important to her emotional growth. She has to disagree with you about *something* in order to have the motivation to move out on her own when she becomes an adult. In other words, if the nest is too cozy, why on earth would she ever want to leave it?

This means that you have to learn not to take it personally when your teen questions, disagrees, or breaks the rules. It's a normal part of her development, not an indictment of your parenting skills or an indication that something is terribly wrong with your relationship with her. In fact, you can look at her learning to think for herself as a compliment to your parenting, knowing that she's not just someone who accepts everything at face value.

Your young adolescent will typically begin to question the "house rules." Any subject is fair game, including rules about visitors, after-school and weekend activities, bedtime, telephone usage, household chores, dating, the need for adult supervision, attending religious activities, and "appropriate" attire. Older teens (and even some younger ones) may also engage parents in conflicts about driving, smoking, drinking alcohol, using illegal drugs, being sexually active, getting a job, dropping out of school, and decisions about whether or not to attend college.

Ideally, a parent will link a teen's privileges to the youngster's demonstration of trustworthiness, good judgment, and increasing responsibility. Realistically, however, this can be a very difficult process. Teens typically push for more freedom and less parental control, often feeling entitled to a privilege just because they are a particular age, are in a particular grade in school, or because they know a peer who has that privilege.

A further complication is that teens notoriously feel invulnerable to danger. "But that won't happen to me!" or "You just don't trust me!" become common teen responses to a parent's concern about realistic issues. What often happens is that a parent will grant a privilege, the teen will test the limits (perhaps using poor judgment), and the parent will have to backtrack and remove the privilege. Since almost no one likes to be told no, is it any wonder that there are so many parent-teen battles?

THE IMPORTANCE OF PEERS

As children move into adolescence, their view of their parents begins to change. Gone are the days of believing that their parents know what's best. In fact, teens quickly become very aware of their parents' biases, problems, and vulnerabilities.

Now a new loyalty evolves as the teen's peer group becomes of primary importance. By learning to relate well to their peers, teens develop the interpersonal skills that will be vital to them as adults. The peer group becomes a testing ground for learning about how other people think, how to communicate effectively, and how to maintain integrity in personal relationships.

The importance of an adolescent's peer group doesn't alter the fact that teens still need their parents (despite their protests to the contrary!). It's just that they need their parents in a different way. They don't need a parent to make so many of their decisions, to think for them, or to be present physically with them as much. But they do need a parent's guidance and mentoring, support and encouragement, and unconditional love. They also need the security of knowing that a parent will step in and set limits for them if they begin participating in activities that are unsafe, irresponsible, or that reflect poor judgment. Teens can say no without losing face with their peers by making a parent "the heavy."

Many parents respond to a teen's shift in loyalty with hurt feelings. They don't realize that it's perfectly normal even for a young teen to spend more time in her room and away from the rest of the family, and to prefer to be with friends rather than parents whenever there's a choice. Although teens will still confide in parents at times (usually of *their* own choosing!), their primary confidants will be their friends.

"I feel like I'm running a boarding house!" is a familiar parental complaint, especially for parents of older teens who have access to a car, who have a job, or who are home from their first year in college. While it might take some creativity, parents can still work out a plan for some individual or family time with a teenager, even if it calls for setting up an appointment well in advance.

Sometimes a parent will try to sabotage a teen's loyalty to the peer group by making a concerted effort to be her buddy or best friend. Whether trying to live vicariously through the teen or simply wanting to avoid the teen's disapproval or rejection, the parent abdicates parental responsibility as a trade-off for staying in the teen's good favor. The problem with this approach is that buddies and friends don't make rules for one another.

While it's certainly desirable, whenever possible, for a parent to have a *friendly rapport* with a teen, that parent also needs to maintain the generational boundary in order to be able to set limits for a teenager when necessary. Too close an attachment to a parent can also interfere with the teen's bonding with peers, hampering her development of necessary interpersonal skills.

EMERGING SEXUALITY

Perhaps one of the most frightening aspects of adolescence for parents is the fact that the teen years signify the arrival of sexuality and reproductive capability. No matter how parents have coped with their own sexual feelings and behavior, they realize that decisions about the expression of sexuality are up to each individual. The fact is that a teenager will make such decisions with or without parental approval, just as parents did themselves.

Typically, a parent wants a teen to view sex as an expression of serious love and commitment, probably in the context of marriage. Yet our media portray sex as everything from a spectator sport to a one-night stand. Many teens become sexually active even in early adolescence, long before they have sufficient maturity for such an emotionally complicated involvement. Concerns about pregnancy and about AIDS and other sexually transmitted diseases can keep a parent awake at night contemplating the *what ifs?* Whether a parent supports a pregnant teen's having an abortion or her having the baby, no parent wants a daughter to face such a choice (or a son to be responsible for a girl's having to make it).

For the teen, emerging sexuality can be scary, exciting, or, most commonly, a mixture of each. Sex is a popular topic among both boys and girls as they compare information, fantasies, and sometimes experiences. Some teens, of course, are too shy to talk about their sexual feelings, and simply listen to their more talkative peers.

It's important that a parent realize how much pressure teenagers are under to have sex, especially older teens. Unless an adolescent is strongly invested in traditional religious or family values that concern premarital sex, he will be very vulnerable to the many messages in our society that teen sex is almost expected.

In America, today's teens live in a society that gives them little parental supervision. At the same time, what they do have is cable television, the Internet, R-rated movies, and college dormitories where eighteen- and nineteen-year-olds are free to sleep with the opposite sex if they so choose. All of this makes it very difficult for an adolescent to resist those hormonal surges!

SEXUAL ORIENTATION

The teen years are also a time when a young person begins to think of himself as a sexual being. This means not only having to deal with raging hormones and worries about being attractive to the opposite sex but also having to grapple with the issue of sexual orientation. Most teens, of course, are attracted to the opposite sex and never give the question of sexual orientation another thought. Some teens, however, anguish about feelings of attraction toward the same sex. Whether such impulses remain in fantasy or are acted upon, the teen is likely to wrestle with their implications.

Some teens in this situation immediately jump to the conclusion that they are homosexual and always will be. They do not realize that many heterosexual adults "experimented" with some sexual behavior with a partner of the same sex during adolescence, perhaps even in same-sex group sexplay. They may not realize that it is possible for a person to be attracted to someone of their own sex as well as to someone of the opposite sex (bisexuality), allowing them a greater sense of choice over their sexual behavior.

Parents understandably are anguished by teens who are not attracted to the opposite sex. Being gay in our society brings with it many difficult struggles, and many people consider it to be a deviant or undesirable lifestyle that is unacceptable for a variety of reasons. Parents may agonize that they have "done something wrong" in their parenting to "cause" a youngster to become homosexual when, in fact, studies have shown that there is no pattern or style of parenting that leads to homosexuality.

TEENS IN LOVE

Young teens are well known for their short-lived crushes and are often labeled "boy crazy" or "girl crazy" by their parents. They will have endless phone conversations with their friends in which the hot topic is who's "going around" or "together" with whom, and who might not "like" them. They will discuss a new romantic interest, plot to get the attention of that person, and then have a friend check to see if the plan has worked. Boy-girl messages are sent via peers rather than being delivered directly. Sometimes, of course, a boy-girl pair become a "couple" to the world of their peers, proclaiming that they are "in love." With young teens, these couplings typically last a few weeks or months. In older teens, relationships may last much longer, and the couple may even begin to talk seriously about a future together. Parents, of course, usually become alarmed about these unions, no matter what the teen's age. They worry that their adolescent is getting way too serious too fast, and become concerned about the possibilty that their teen is or might soon become sexually active.

It's important for parents to understand that teen love is too important to be discounted as "puppy love." The adolescent's feelings are usually very genuine and deep. While the relationship might be seen as "immature" from an adult perspective, it is only because the adult is no longer in the teen's emotional shoes. Consequently, a parent can greatly damage an otherwise good relationship with a teen by making light of the intensity or integrity of the adolescent's feelings of romantic love.

HOW MUCH EDUCATION?

Although there are many exceptions, a person usually has greater career and economic opportunities the more education she has. Consequently, many parents become very concerned about their teen's academic achievement in high school, wanting their adolescent to qualify for admission to a good college.

Some of the biggest and most emotional parent-teen battles occur over the subject of school attendance, homework, and grades. Especially frustrating for the parent is the adolescent who has terrific potential but who is totally unmotivated to do schoolwork.

Some teens, eager to get out on their own and/or fed up with pressure about school, elect to drop out of high school. Parents sometimes find themselves having to walk a fine line between encouraging their teen to continue an education and not pushing them into further rebellion about academics.

PREPARATION FOR A JOB OR CAREER

An important developmental task for the older adolescent is to begin to form some idea of how she will support herself as an adult, preferably in a way that she will enjoy. It's not that she must know the *specific* job or career she might want. Rather it's a time for her to gain a sense of what's important to her about the kind of work she will do. If she's clear about her criteria for the ideal job/career, it will be much easier for her to find a suitable occupation. Parents can help in this matter by posing a number of critical questions to their older teen. Is it more important for her to

- Work with people, or work with things?
- Have a set routine, or have a flexible schedule?
- Spend most of her time in a building, or most of her time outdoors?
- Be fairly sedentary, or be quite physically active?
- Be highly creative, or follow a prescribed structure or routine?
- Be in a position of control or leadership, or let someone else make the rules?
- Work independently, or work with a team?
- Be more of a "big picture" person, or be a detail person?
- Work in a job that stays about the same from year to year, or work on one project and then move on to one that is totally different?
- Be the person who initiates a particular goal, or be the person who follows through, or both?
- Be competitive, or be noncompetitive?
- Be service oriented, or be sales oriented?
- Have a set salary, on work on commission?

In addition to thinking about such preferences, a teen will also need to consider some other factors: how much education she will need (and her willingness to obtain it), how much money she will have to make to support the lifestyle she wants to have, whether she has a need for staus or recognition, and whether or not the work she chooses will be compatible with other goals she might have (to travel, to have children, and so on). Obviously, it is also critical that the work she chooses will mesh with her specific talents and capabilities.

There are some teens who know from an early age what they want to do "when they grow up." The majority, however, will form their ideas about this somewhere between mid-adolescence and their early or mid twenties. While it's helpful for parents to get an older teen to begin *thinking* about the job/career criteria that are important to the adolescent, it's also important that parents make it clear it's okay for teens *not to know* all their criteria. Parents sometimes pressure a teen to "get serious about your life and figure out what you want to do with it" too soon, creating unnecessary anxiety and/or resentment in everyone. In response to pressure, a teen may choose too soon—or opt out by not moving in any direction—compounding everyone's anxirty and unhappiness.

Instead, it's helpful for parents to encourage their teens to consider many options, and to take their time to allow a genuine job/career interest to blossom. Adolescents who are ambivalent about going to college often do better if they take a break from school for a year or two, allowing themselves some time to mature. Some older teens will opt for joining the military service or an organization such as the Peace Corps after they graduate from high school. Some want to prepare for specific vocations that require schooling, but not a four-year college degree. It's also amazing to see how motivated for college a young person can become after supporting herself in a minimum-wage job for a while!

Parents who are disappointed with their older teen's decisions—or lack of them—about these matters need to remember that today's adolescents will probably not select one job or career and then stick with it until retirement. The world and the economy they will enter is tumultuous and fast-changing. It's very likely that they will have several jobs or careers as they continue to grow throughout their life span. Giving teens the message that they will evolve physically, mentally, emotionally, and spiritually as they live their lives creates the exciting and realistic expectation that life is always full of possibilities, choices, and changes.

WHAT'S COMING UP?

The parent of a teen has a complicated and sobering job. There is a lot happening in a young person's life now, and parents need to understand that as fully as possible. But they also need to look at what's happening in their own lives. We all bring our present circumstances, anxieties, and concerns to our decision making. The better you understand the conflicts of your stage in life, the more constructive you will be as you greet the challenges of guiding your adolescent.

T W O

WHAT'S REALLY
HAPPENING WITH PARENTS
OF TEENS?

When you think about having a teenager around the house, the thoughts that run through your mind are likely to be about the kinds of behavior for which adolescents are so well known: mood swings, rebellion, testing the rules, emotional displays, sexual urges, increased peer influence, and so on. Who wouldn't feel a bit daunted by these probabilities?

Yet this view leaves out a key factor that can make parenting an adolescent so challenging: Parents are going through their *own* developmental stages. Whatever is going on in a parent's own psychological/emotional stage of life has a great impact on how that parent reacts to whatever is going on with the teen!

To get a clearer idea about the interplay between parents and teens, consider first the age of the parent. The age of most parents of adolescents falls somewhere within the late twenties to the late fifties, the bulk probably being in their late thirties or late forties. In other words, the majority of parents of teens are either approaching, entering, or fully in the period known as midlife.

Consider the kinds of issues people in midlife are facing. For most, it's a time of reassessment in which they take a long, hard look at their lives. They consider what they have achieved in their jobs or careers, and in their marriages or other significant relationships. They also look at what they *haven't* accomplished. They may begin to question the meaning of their lives, if they haven't already done so, and to search for a personal philosophy about the world and about their place in it. For many, it's a time for making decisions about either recommitting to their current course or changing their direction.

Some parents of teens find themselves coping with a recent or impending divorce during midlife. This is usually an extremely painful time for everyone concerned—adults and teens alike—but it is especially so for the mother or father who is being divorced against his or her will. Parents' problems are compounded by the emotional upheaval that comes from the adjustment problems so typical of teens and younger children who are going through this family crisis.

Midlife is also a time when many adults are faced with, or soon will be confronted with, having to care for ill or elderly parents. Or perhaps one or both of their parents have died. They might have health problems of their own, and perhaps they have experienced the death of a close peer. Such realities can take their emotional toll, and they typically bring about an awareness of one's own mortality.

Given this backdrop, let's look at how parents might react to their teenager.

COMMON PARENT RESPONSES

As we examine some common parent reactions to teens, you'll notice that some relate to midlife issues, others to the parent's own personal history. Remember that these influences might be totally out of a parent's conscious awareness. Bringing them out into the open allows a parent to have a greater understanding of the dynamics at play, as well as offering more choices in handling such feelings.

"OH, TO BE YOUNG AGAIN"

Just at the stage when you may be snipping out gray hairs, working out to debag and desag yourself, and attacking your cellulite and wrinkles with a vengeance, here comes your adolescent with a seemingly near-perfect body. Your teen is likely to be slender and toned and might even be blessed with certain physical characteristics that you always dreamed of having. He may have the height that you always wanted in order to be able to play basketball; she might have the cleavage that you could only badly imitate with padding. Just when you've decided never again to appear publicly in shorts, your teen is looking fantastic in a bikini. The point is a parent can't help but compare his or her body with that of a same-sexed teen, and the result can be pretty painful.

And look at that budding sexuality! If you are uncomfortable with your past sexual behavior—or with your own current sexuality—you probably don't want your teenager to follow in your footsteps. Or you might envy today's sexual freedom, especially if you feel you missed out on the so-called sexual revolution. Even if you are comfortable with your sexuality, you are well aware of the consequences that can face those who make poor sexual choices. No matter what, sex is typically worrisome for parents of adolescents.

Although your teen might feel that his life is terribly difficult, you're likely to view it as quite the opposite. It might seem nice to go back to a seven-hour school day, to get to sleep until noon on weekends, to have cleaning your room and maybe taking out the trash twice a week as your only chores, and to be able to chat with your friends for hours on end. When your teen complains about his torturous life, you may want to tell him, "Just wait till you have bills, taxes, long work hours, unappreciative kids, and no longer get the Christmas holidays, spring break, and all summer off!"

If your older teen begins to consider his options for college, you might envy the fun and excitement of anticipating such a step. You might also envy the sheer amount of choice that's available to him these days. When you went to college, did you have a computer available that could give you the nitty-gritty details about the physical facilities, academic programs, and social features of every college available? Could you get credit for racquetball or aerobics instead of those garden-variety physical education classes? Could you have lived in a coed dormitory, with virtually no rules?

The same feeling of unlimited choices also holds for occupations and careers your son or daughter might wish to pursue. Almost all of them are open to both sexes, and there's no longer a concern about making just one choice and having to stick with it the rest of one's life. The more you felt pressured by circumstances or by family to embark on the job or career path you're taking presently, the more likely you are to feel a little jealous of your teen's freedom in this regard.

How are such feelings likely to affect your parenting? If you're willing to acknowledge your own feelings of envy, at least you can carefully examine the parenting decisions you make in the areas that tap into such feelings. If such feelings are denied, however, you're more likely to react unreasonably or irrationally to your teen.

For example, if you conceived a child out of wedlock, you might be overly vigilant about your daughter's sexual behavior, possibly setting rigid, unrealistic limits on her regarding dating, curfews, and so on. Such actions might only encourage your daughter's rebellion in this area, making it more possible that the very thing you most fear will actually occur.

Or take the situation where you feel envious of your teen's free time and seeming lack of responsibility. You might react by rigidly demanding that he fill his time with a myriad of chores, making it almost impossible for him to have the normal socialization experiences he needs. Your teen might react by consciously or unconsciously getting back at you in some way, perhaps through low grades or by trying to involve you in endless power struggles over those chores.

The point is it's normal to feel a little envious of your teenager. However, most adults will tell you that they would never actually trade places with their teen even if such a thing were possible. It is the perspective offered by one's own maturity that allows adults to see aspects of the teenage years that can't be appreciated by those who are in the midst of them.

If you find yourself overly envious or preoccupied with jealous feelings toward your teen, it's wise to take a look at what might be missing in your own life. Focusing on the true source of your unhappiness will allow you to redirect your energies and will make it less likely that such feelings about your teen will get in the way of your parenting.

"PLEASE, DON'T LET ME REPEAT WHAT MY PARENTS DID!"

Many of us grow up vowing to be different from our parents in some specific way. Whether they were too strict and didn't allow us any free time, nagged us incessantly about our schoolwork, insisted we go to bed too early, wouldn't allow us to have friends over to spend the night, or wouldn't let us spend our allowance as we saw fit, we hated their policy and are determined that we won't make the same mistake with our own offspring.

The problem is sometimes the pendulum swings to the opposite extreme, and we become either too permissive or too strict. Suddenly, we wake up and realize that we're behaving just as outrageously as our parents did, albeit in the other direction!

We also don't want our teenagers to repeat the painful experiences we may have had when we were adolescents. Wanting to protect them from hurt, danger, or embarrassment, we may become overly protective, overly permissive, or utterly inconsistent with them. Striking the right balance can be difficult when our teens get themselves into situations that automatically rubber-band us back into our own similar experiences when we were adolescents.

If you become aware that an emotional issue from your past is being triggered by your teen's behavior or attitude and that you are responding unreasonably or irrationally, consult a mental health professional. Not only can you get help resolving an old personal issue, but you'll also be in a better position to respond more appropriately to your teen.

"I JUST DON'T LIKE CONFLICT!"

If you have a nonconfrontive personality, you might find it especially difficult to deal effectively with your teenager. Because adolescents are notorious for arguing, testing, and even badgering their parents to get what they want, it takes persistence, energy, and assertiveness to hang in there and deal with a situation.

Parents who are afraid that a teen will get mad at them, perhaps even reject them for a while, are particularly vulnerable to catering to an adolescent's demands. They just can't bear the thought that their offspring is not loving and appreciative of them. The teenager, of course, quickly picks up on this dynamic and manipulates such parents into giving her carte blanche to do as she wishes.

Interestingly, adults whose parents followed the passive route with them when they were teens will frequently tell you that they very much resent their parents' not having had the courage to stand up to them. Even some insightful older teens will also admit such feelings about their overly permissive parents. The point is that effective parents refuse to be manipulated. They stand up to an adolescent who's being unreasonable or who wants to do something that is dangerous or that shows poor judgment. In spite of her loud protestations to the contrary, the teenager gets the message that such parents genuinely care about her.

If you find that you are squeamish about facing conflict with your adolescent because you will feel hurt by her anger at you, it's helpful to remember that an adolescent needs to know that your relationship bond is strong enough to withstand her—and your—anger at each another. Keep in mind, also, that she's learning that anger occurs in emotionally intimate relationships, and that neither person needs to keep himself in a one-down position by acquiescing consistently to the other's wishes.

"DO WHAT I SAY, OR ELSE!"

Equally ineffective as parents who give in to a teen out of a wish not to create conflict are parents who must always have control. Such parents feel threatened by a teen's disagreeing with them and often react to an adolescent's requests or demands by rigidly insisting that she do exactly as she's told. Compromise or negotiation are seen as undesirable and viewed as a challenge to the parents' rightful control.

Successfully parenting a teen requires allowing an adolescent to take more control over her decisions as she matures, taking back control when necessary, and then relinquishing it again as the teen demonstrates increasing responsibility and judgment. Parents who refuse to give up any control and maintain a highly authoritarian position often produce teens who are outright rebellious. The other option for the adolescent is to become submissive out of fear of parental disapproval or wrath. Such teens often become overly dependent, unable to make decisions for themselves when they get to be adults. Others become masters of passive aggression, seemingly cooperative on the surface while harboring deep resentments within and getting back at the parents in subtle ways. While an adolescent's submission to parental authority results in less open conflict around the house, it doesn't allow her to develop the skills for assertiveness or for independent thinking that she'll need as an adult.

"HELP! I'M LOSING MY CHILD!"

The transition from parenting a child to parenting a teen can be jarring, to say the least. "What happened to that sweet little kid I knew?" is a familiar parental lament. Suddenly, there's more conflict, and the trouble teens can get into seems monumental compared with the issues you worried about with your young child.

Even more upsetting for many parents, however, is the adolescent's development into a young adult. You spend eighteen years or so trying to "raise" your offspring, and suddenly the course of your teen's life seems out of your hands. Whatever control you once had is now gone. For better or for worse, the job is almost finished. Your teen still needs you, but in a different way.

What you hope for, of course, is that your adult "child" will still love and care about you and that he'll want to continue a relationship with you. You want him to like you as a person and to look forward to talking with you and visiting with you. You don't want him to dread having to come visit you on holidays, or just to make a "token" call on Mother's or Father's Day, strictly out of a sense of obligation.

To be healthy, your relationship with your adult "child" will evolve into one between equals in which control will no longer be an issue. For this process to occur, you'll need to relate to your new adult in a different way. If you're wise, you'll only give your opinion when asked. You'll be honest but noncritical; supportive but nonintrusive. You'll be eager and enthusiastic to see him, but never make him feel guilty for choosing to do something other than to visit you. You will accept the fact that he will fulfill his own destiny via the choices he makes and that those choices are his responsibility, not yours.

By following these principles, your reward is likely to be a loving, close bond with your adult "child," even if you are separated physically by great distance. Although you will be equals in one sense, there will still be a special quality to your relationship that only exists between parents and their children of any age.

If you find yourself feeling miserable or depressed when your older teen leaves home (beyond those normal first pangs of "empty nest" sadness), use this as a signal that there is room in your life for some other interest or challenge. You are entering a new phase of your own development, and now is the perfect time to do whatever it is you've always wanted to do but couldn't while you had to respond to the demands of parenting. Perhaps it will be a new job or career, a creative endeavor, the fulfillment of a desire to travel, an intriguing project, a renewed emotional investment in your marriage, or a time for spiritual pursuits.

WHEN PARENTS DISAGREE

Unfortunately, the picture of two parents who are in consistent agreement about how to handle parenting issues may be more an illusion than a reality. Dealing with a child can precipitate serious conflict between parents, making children one of the greatest stressors on even the best of marriages.

In many cases, two parents will polarize on particular issues. One feels their fourteen-year-old daughter is old enough to begin dating; the other insists that she can't date until she's seventeen. One thinks it's okay for teens to drink alcohol so long as they don't begin abusing it; the other thinks it's outrageous to consider allowing a teen to drink until he's of legal age. One feels that a sexually active daughter should be given birth control pills; the other insists that the daughter should refrain from sexual activity and that allowing her birth control only gives a teen permission to be sexually active.

One thing is for sure: If there's a spark of disagreement between two parents, a teenager will manage to find and exploit it. Consequently, parents who don't agree on an issue are often put to a severe test, especially on those matters that tap into their basic values and belief systems.

Therapists who work with teens and their families will tell you that the adolescents who get into the most trouble are those whose parents remain polarized on critical parenting issues. In such cases, they will often counsel the parents to let *one parent* set all rules for the teen, as parental inconsistency is the worst scenario. Even though the chosen parent might be far too strict or too lenient according to parenting experts, it is the *consistency* of parental expectation that is most important in keeping the teenager from escalating the problem.

The ideal situation is for parents who seriously disagree to get help from a mental health professional. If some negotiation between viewpoints isn't possible, it is likely to be suggested that one parent take total charge of rule setting and discipline for a particular teen.

Admittedly, single parents have a tough time when they are the primary full-time parent. Parenting can be exhausting, confusing, and frustrating, especially when children become teenagers and begin to push for more control over their lives. Having the other parent present to share the responsibility of tough decisions, not to mention offering physical and emotional support, is a tremendous advantage.

In spite of all this, single parents do have one distinct advantage over two-parent households: the avoidance of parental conflict.

Rather than having to struggle with a spouse who doesn't agree about a particular issue, the single parent can make unilateral decisions where rules and discipline of a teen are concerned. Considering the number of parents whose marriages can come apart at the seams over such conflicts, the ability of a parent to implement his or her own values and beliefs, often without much opposition, can be viewed as an advantage. Of course, a disagreeing ex-spouse can set up a power struggle with the parent in charge, perhaps vying for a teen's favor in the process.

There are also single parents who are unable to set limits on their teens. These adults simply acquiesce to their teenagers' demands, allowing themselves to be manipulated. In a two-parent household, the likelihood is greater that one parent will be able to set privileges and enforce consequences, providing emotional support for the weaker parent and consequently creating an atmosphere of parental consistency and agreement.

THE REMARRIED PARENT

One of the most challenging and difficult situations arises when a parent of a teen has remarried. While younger children *may* be more accepting of a stepparent, many teens resent a new influence coming into the home. Even if they like the stepparent, they balk against him or her as a rule setter or enforcer. If they don't like the stepparent, things can get even worse. The teen's "I don't have to listen to him (her)!" is an almost certain occurrence, either way.

Because of the complexity of the problems in stepfamilies and blended families, it is highly recommended that parents educate themselves about the issues that typically arise in such situations (see "Suggested Reading" section) or consult with a mental health professional who deals with such problems. It's a common occurrence for such marriages to break up because of the severe stress any child, but particularly a teenager, can place on the couple's new relationship.

A FINAL THOUGHT

If you're feeling a bit sad that your active parenting days are over, you may find consolation in the words of Kahlil Gibran:

*And a woman who held a babe against her bosom said, Speak to us
of Children.
And he said:
Your children are not your children.
They are the sons and daughters of Life's longing for itself.
They come through you but not from you,
And though they are with you yet they belong not to you.
You may give them your love but not your thoughts,
For they have their own thoughts.
You may house their bodies but not their souls,
For their souls dwell in the house of tomorrow, which you
cannot visit, not even in your dreams.
You may strive to be like them, but seek not to make them
like you.
For life goes not backward nor tarries with yesterday.
You are the bows from which your children as living arrows
are sent forth.
The archer sees the mark upon the path of the infinite, and
He bends you with His might that His arrows may go swift and far.
Let your bending in the archer's hand be for gladness;
For even as He loves the arrow that flies, so He loves also
the bow that is stable.**

THREE

"CAN WE TALK?"

Probably the most common complaint, from both teenagers and their parents, is "We just can't communicate!" Somehow, there has been a shutdown, and once it occurs, both generations tend to be pessimistic about the possibility of fixing it. As you might expect, this situation only makes whatever conflicts arise even more difficult to resolve.

In this chapter, you'll learn some practical dos and don'ts to help you keep those lines of communication open with your teen so that a major "shutdown" doesn't occur. You'll get some tips on how to talk, when to talk, and how to listen to your adolescent. You'll be forewarned about common ways you might unintentionally block communication, especially in those sensitive situations when your values are threatened or when your teen habitually takes the opposite position from your own. You'll see how to deal with your teen's breaking rules and how to negotiate a behavior contract. And you'll learn some tips for disciplining your teen when necessary.

HOW TO TALK TO YOUR TEEN

The ideal way to talk to your teenager is to remain calm and matter-of-fact, showing respect for your adolescent's ideas while clearly and nondefensively stating your own views. *Sounds terrific*, you might say to yourself, *but how do I manage to keep my emotions in check?* After all, it's common knowledge that adolescents can be masters at pulling a parent's emotional chain!

It's true that you are likely to face times when you'll feel furious, frustrated, hurt, or overwhelmed when you try to discuss an issue with your teen. Rather than blowing up (and acting like a tantruming two-year-old in a grown-up suit), it's best to give yourself a time-out to cool off and collect your thoughts.

It's okay to say something to your teen such as, "I'm so upset that I don't want to discuss this matter right now. Let's talk about this after dinner tonight (or in half an hour)." At that point, either ask your teen to go to her room or *you* leave the room, depending on the circumstances.

This same tactic also applies to your teenager. If she's behaving inappropriately, such as yelling at you or making rude remarks, let her know that she's too upset for a discussion and ask her to go to her room until she's ready to talk calmly and respectfully to you. However, she must talk to you when she comes out of her room, or at some designated time, rather than just ignoring the issue. If she refuses, she can be grounded from her privileges until she agrees to discuss the matter calmly, or perhaps she could be allowed to negotiate a time in the near future when she will agree to discuss it.

If your conversations with your teen frequently get heated and out of control, you'll need to make an agreement about this mutual time-out policy. Many teens say that their parents will not let them have time to cool down and that if the teen goes to her room, the parent follows and continues the discussion. Some of the worst confrontations occur in such a situation, with tempers rapidly escalating.

Parents, of course, state that they *must* follow a teen to her room, otherwise she will never finish the original discussion. The solution is for both parent and teen to agree on a win-win arrangement: The parent agrees to leave the adolescent alone to cool down; the teen agrees that, having cooled down, she will return to the parent to finish the discussion.

WHEN TO TALK TO YOUR TEEN

A problem that often arises when a parent wants to talk to a teen has to do with timing. It seems that just when a parent is about ready for bed, a teen will suddenly want to talk. After all, she's spent the earlier part of the evening talking with her friends and/ or doing homework. Parents seem to be the last choice. Unfair as this may seem, the fact is that unless a parent makes time available when a teen is ready to talk, chances are the teen will just clam up and not attempt to communicate. It's a matter of seizing a golden opportunity. The wise parent will sacrifice a little sleep in order to allow such moments to occur.

This is not to say that a parent should never refuse to talk at a teen's request. Obviously, parents have commitments to keep and times when they feel emotionally drained or physically unable to concentrate on conversation. The point is it's best to keep your refusals to talk to a minimum and, when they do occur, to arrange a specified time to talk just as soon as possible after the initial request.

With today's busy lifestyles, many parents feel at a loss to find time to talk to a teen, not for confrontations about issues but just to catch up, to share, and to strengthen the parent-teen bond. When the parent has free time, the teen might be in school, studying, or involved with friends.

An ideal time for most parents and teens to have some one-on-one time is to go out together for a meal. In this situation you have a captive audience; there can be no excuses about homework to do, friends who drop in unexpectedly, phone calls to interrupt, household chores that can't wait, or other family members who interfere.

A lunch on the weekend, or dinner anytime, is nice, if you can arrange it. However, many families have more than one child/teen and might find it difficult to take one youngster to dinner and leave another at home. Believe it or not, breakfast is often the ideal time. Most teens like the idea, once they get over the trauma of having to get up a little earlier. Going out for breakfast usually doesn't take time away from your work or from her school, and adolescents aren't known for making social plans early in the morning. Since a parent's going out for breakfast with a teen is unusual in many families, the teen feels complimented and made special by this obvious break in routine.

Teens are also prone to talking with a parent while the two are riding alone in a car, providing neither party is angry at the other. If you find that you never seem to get time to talk alone with your teen, consider taking advantage of this opportunity by inviting her to accompany you on errands, shopping, and so on. If either a mall or a meal is included in the activity, you'll be more likely to have the honor of an adolescent's company!

HOW TO LISTEN TO YOUR TEEN

Parents sometimes forget that talking is only one side of communication; equally important is listening! Both teenagers and parents commonly protest that the other party "never listens to me."

Typically, parents *think* they're listening when, in fact, they are not giving the teen enough time to explain himself. The teen makes a remark, and the parent jumps in with advice, disagreement, protestations, facts to consider, or an interpretation of what the teen must "really" think.

The secret of listening, and of having the other person feel *listened to*, is to hang back a little rather than jumping in with all ten toes! Instead of trying to convince a teen of anything, simply *reflect back* what the teen seems to be feeling. Comments like "You seem upset. What happened?" or "Gosh, you sound really angry. Tell me more about it," or "What went wrong? You seem really frustrated" encourage your teen to continue talking, giving you a better opportunity to understand what's really going on.

This kind of listening has been called *active listening*, and there are two distinct advantages to learning to use it. First, you are likely to get much more information from your teen. Second, the teen is more likely to think through the situation, coming up with his own solution to the problem, if there is one. When this happens, you are in a great position to praise your adolescent for his clear thinking and/or good judgment, increasing his confidence in his ability to solve his own problems or, perhaps, to calm himself down.

COMMUNICATION BLOCKERS

Now let's take a look at some of the ways parents typically, albeit unintentionally, shut down the lines of communication with their teenagers.

LECTURING

If there's one thing that will turn an adolescent off completely, it's a lecture. Adolescents' eyes glaze over when parents launch into lengthy explanations in an attempt to get the teen to see a different point of view. Because a parent senses that the teen has turned off, or simply disagrees, the adult typically tries to get a point across by saying the same thing over again or by citing more examples, probably increasing voice volume at the same time.

The fact is that lectures not only shut down communication, they just don't change anything. When used as a method of discipline, they are usually totally ineffective. Teens will frankly tell their friends, "No, I didn't get grounded. I just had to listen to my mom's lecture for half an hour! Big deal!"

To prevent yourself from lecturing, pause often as you are explaining your viewpoint and wait for feedback, or at least for some acknowledgment. If he's totally uncooperative, refusing to listen or to participate in a discussion with you, ask him to go to his room until he's ready to discuss the matter, or agree to talk at a specific time later in the day. It will do you no good to harangue or yell at him; the only likely effect will be to alienate your teen more and/or to raise your own blood pressure!

ARGUING

Parents often bitterly complain that their teenagers argue with them incessantly. While this may be true, the teenager is only half of the problem. The parent has to be arguing, too, since it's impossible to have an argument all by yourself (unless it's inside your own head, in which case it doesn't bother anybody else).

The kind of arguments we're talking about are those in which a parent has taken a clear stance but the teen continues to invite further discussion by badgering the parent with endless repetition, rehashing the same things over and over. Adolescents continue to do this, of course, because they have learned that a parent will eventually cave in and acquiesce to the teen's position. The parent realizes later—or perhaps even while the argument is going on—that she's being manipulated, but feels helpless to take control of the situation.

This frustrating experience can be curtailed by a parent's simply refusing to argue. Once both parties have stated their viewpoints and rationales, and a parent has made a decision, the discussion needs to end. Instead of continuing to counter the teen's challenges, a parent can say something like "I've made my decision, and I'm not going to discuss the same topic any more," or "That's it. Discussion's over!" Then comes the critical part: refusing to talk any more about the issue *even if the teen continues talking*! If a parent allows herself the luxury of one last remark in response to something the teen has said, that parent is unwittingly encouraging the teen to continue arguing.

Many parents find this advice hard to accept, feeling that it's important to their sense of parental authority to have uttered the last word. However, the "last word" really means nothing and is a false victory. Parents have all kinds of leverage with teenagers by being able to grant or remove their privileges, such as using the telephone, playing a stereo, going out on weekends, driving a car, and so on. It is this leverage that gives a parent control, not the utterance of words.

VALUES AND CAUSES

One of the most difficult parent-teen confrontations can occur when an adolescent questions a parent's basic values, or gets caught up in a passionate cause that fills the parent with shock or dismay. Ironically, the more upset the parent becomes, the more the teen might stubbornly dig in and maintain what the parent considers to be a totally outrageous position.

Many parents respond to these situations by angrily expressing outright disapproval. Some attempt to make the teenager feel guilty by saying things like "How could any son of mine ever even *think* such a thing!" or "Where did I go wrong as a mother?" or "After all I've done for you, and this is the way I get repaid!" As you might imagine, such responses only alienate the teen further.

When you find yourself in such a situation, resist the urge to give an immediate opinion or emotional reaction. Instead, put those "active listening" skills into action. Express a calm curiosity about why your adolescent thinks the way he does, saying something like "Really? I'm curious to know more about that," or "Well, tell me how you've decided that." Then simply listen to your teen with as much objectivity as you can muster.

After you've heard your teen's viewpoint, express your own. Of course, it's possible that you could end up agreeing with him. More likely, you'll still disagree, but now is your opportunity to get across your own view. If there is a point your teen has expressed that you can agree with, be sure to mention that first. Then explain your position, but without putting down his remarks as "crazy," "stupid," "immature," or "ridiculous." If you become judgmental at this point, you'll blow the rapport you've already established.

By first *listening respectfully* to your adolescent's feelings and thoughts, he'll be much more receptive to listening to yours. This allows you the important opportunity to clarify your own values, and perhaps to broaden your teen's perspective. This tactic doesn't guarantee that your adolescent will end up agreeing with you in the long run, but it makes the possibility much more likely. And at least you'll feel you had the chance to make your opinions known.

THE DEVIL'S ADVOCATE

Realize that many times when your teen argues a position that you find intolerable or infuriating, the fact that you can't get her to agree with you after the most calm and reasoned discussion doesn't *necessarily* mean that she *doesn't* agree with you. Adolescents are well known for playing the devil's advocate. They will staunchly maintain a position just to get a parent's reaction, perhaps secretly wanting to hear your reasoning in order to resolve their own ambivalence. Besides, teens frequently resist acknowledging that a parent might be right! However, if you could become invisible at another time in a room where your adolescent is discussing the same issue with a friend, you might be surprised to hear her recounting *your* views as her own.

THE POLARITY RESPONSE

Similar to the devil's-advocate position, but motivated by a different dynamic, is the polarity response. This describes the reaction of a person who automatically *polarizes* to whatever position the other person takes; for example, if you say it's too cold, the polarity responder says it's too warm; if you say something is black, the polarizer says it's only gray.

Realize that the reason a person develops a polarity response is that he is trying to preserve his right to choose for himself. He is probably not aware of this dynamic, but unconsciously he doesn't want to feel that another person is controlling his decisions or opinions. Since adolescents are at the developmental stage where they are fighting to establish their independence from authority figures, you can see how parents of teens are likely to be all too familiar with the polarity response!

Obviously, you don't change a polarity responder by trying to convince him of the error in his thinking. Instead, appeal to his underlying wish to choose for himself. For example, you might say something like "Well, don't take my word for it, Sam, but *ask your-self* if it's really best for you to take that chemistry class next se-mester instead of study hall. You want to figure out what makes the best sense to *you*." Or if you are suggesting that he do something specific, try saying, "Sam, you might want to read that book to prepare yourself for the SAT, or you might not." The fact that you've added the "or you might not" makes it impossible for Sam to polarize to you, since you've already given him permission *not* to follow your advice! Just using these simple communication tactics can greatly reduce those power struggles for which parents and teens are so famous.

WHEN RULES ARE BROKEN

When your teen begins to question house rules or tests limits by breaking the ones that are already established, it's a good idea to sit down with him and discuss the situation rather than engage in repeated arguments when the matter comes up again. It's best not to have this discussion at a time when emotions are high, but rather when everyone is calm.

Listen to your teen's point of view first, even if you feel that the issue will probably remain nonnegotiable. If you think your teen is correct, tell him so and allow him to go by the policy he's requesting. If you think it's unwise to go along with his suggestion but that some compromise is possible, explain your position and negotiate a new plan. If you are unwilling to change your position in any way, tell him so, as well as the reasons for your decision.

Because it is important that a teenager feel increasing control over his own life, try to negotiate on all but the most important issues. In other words, carefully pick your battles, standing firm on the "biggies" (safety, health, ethics, legal issues, and so on) and allowing compromise on those issues that are more a matter of personal preference.

If your teen begins to question a number of your rules, it's helpful to establish a "contract." Typically, this would involve specifying rules about the teen's household responsibilities, phone use, curfews, having guests, and after-school or weekend activities.

Included in the contract are the *privileges* the teen can earn for following the contract, as well as the *consequences* he will experience when he doesn't follow it.

When setting up this kind of contract, it's helpful first to discuss the general idea of it with the adolescent and then ask *him* to draw up the first draft. Since it is a well-known fact that people are more likely to follow through with something when they have had some input into it, your teen will be more receptive to the whole contract idea by getting the opportunity to design it. If his "first draft" is acceptable, you have an opportunity to compliment him for his judgment and clear thinking; if parts of it are outrageous or unacceptable, stand firm on the points that aren't negotiable and compromise on the ones that are.

If your teen asks for a privilege that you don't think he's quite ready for, consider spelling out the conditions under which you *would* allow him to have it. For example, if he wants a much later curfew, you might tell him that you will renegotiate a *somewhat* later curfew after a certain time period, gradually making the curfew later based on his demonstrated willingness to follow the current contract.

While it might seem silly, it's a good idea to write down a contract that involves a number of areas of concern (phone rules, curfews, chores, and so on). Ask everyone involved to sign it. Then *make a copy* for your teen and agree to abide by it for a certain minimum time period. The contract should not be changed on impulse, especially after an argument about it, but opportunities for renegotiation can be set up at appropriate time intervals.

Having a contract is a way of demonstrating to a teenager that he *does* have choices and *is* responsible for those choices. By agreeing to specific criteria for his privileges and consequences, his not fulfilling the contract is clearly the result of his own choices. Rather than his privileges being taken away because of an emotional or subjective decision on the part of a parent, the teen can see that it was his choice to forfeit the privilege. Instead of being the heavy, a parent can actually behave as the teen's advocate; for example, "Let's see, Brent, it looks like your not cleaning your room by the time we agreed each week is what's keeping you from getting your maximum allowance. How do you think you can remember to get this done next week so that you'll get the money you need for that jacket you want to buy?"

WHEN YOU NEED TO DISCIPLINE YOUR TEEN

Physical discipline, such as spanking or any kind of hitting, is definitely inappropriate for an adolescent. The emotional hurt and rage it fosters in a teenager runs deep and exacerbates the teen's normal resentments toward parental control. There's just something insulting about being hit or slapped, especially when you are expected not to fight back! Actually, a teen is much more likely than a younger child to fight back physically with a parent, especially when his physical size becomes equal to or larger than the adult's. The scuffling that ensues can result in physical harm to one or both parties.

The two most effective negative consequences for an adolescent are *loss of privileges* and *restriction*. These two consequences are actually on a continuum, with restriction typically involving the loss of several privileges for a more serious offense.

Perhaps the most common error parents make in implementing these negative consequences is that they set the penalty for too long a period. If a parent takes away a privilege for too long, the teen may commit some other offense before the privilege is earned back. If several offenses occur within a few weeks' time, the parent will quickly run out of privileges to take away. Also, a teen can easily feel defeated if too much is taken away for too long, developing the "who cares, anyway!" attitude that is self-defeating for the adolescent and infuriating for the parent.

If you need to impose the more serious discipline of restriction, be especially careful about the terms. It is important to be very clear about when the restriction will end, either by setting a specified period (e.g., twenty-four hours or one week) or by setting a specified criterion (e.g., when the teen brings a note from the English teacher stating that he has caught up on all missing assignments, or when he has cleaned his room to specification). If either the time limit or the criterion are unspecified or vague, your teen is likely to have little motivation to improve. As an example, consider the common parental statement "You're grounded until you change your attitude!" The teen thinks, *Does this mean I've blown it if I give her one dirty look? This will be impossible! Why try, anyway?*

If you find it necessary to set a lengthy restriction, say two to three weeks or more, it's best to allow your teen to earn back *something* each week of the restriction. For example, "You may not go out with your friends for three weeks, but you can have your phone privileges back in one week if you clean up your room." Or, "You can have the television back in your room if you are passing all your courses at the end of the grading period; however, I'll check with the school counselor in two weeks, and if she reports that your teachers are seeing improvement in your effort, you can have your TV back on the weekends."

Sometimes you might find yourself in the awkward position of having set a totally unreasonable restriction ("You're grounded until the end of *next* semester!") or of setting one that you later realize will punish *you* ("You can cancel your plans to stay at Bob's house this weekend and just stay home," then realizing that you have plans to be out of town all weekend!). Rather than letting things slide by not enforcing the restriction (but not telling your teen that you changed your mind either), it's best to admit your mistake. Tell your teen that you were upset and acted hastily or unreasonably; then set an appropriate restriction for the offense.

As long as your teen's behavior justifies a negative consequence, resist the temptation to cancel an entire restriction just because you made a mistake. When an adolescent experiences frequent inconsistency in your enforcement of the consequences you set for him, he won't take you seriously in the future ("My dad has me on restriction, but don't worry, he always forgets about it!"). When this happens, you've lost both your credibility and your leverage.

A HELPFUL ATTITUDE

When talking and listening to your teenager, don't let yourself become so self-conscious about these rules of thumb that you wind up tongue-tied and give up communicating before you've started. Remember, these tips represent ideals that you can strive for, but nobody's going to get it perfect all the time.

The important point is that there are better and worse ways to talk to teens. If you think you're having problems communicating, you can now pinpoint some problem areas and then try something different. And if you blow it on occasion, there will be ample opportunities for correction!

PART II
MORE
SPECIFICALLY . . .

F O U R

FRIENDSHIPS

Like it or not, your teen's peer group becomes an important key to her emerging independence. Rather than looking to you, her parent, as her primary authority, she'll now begin actively to seek out the opinions and advice of other teens. She's much more likely to value their opinions over yours, viewing you as old-fashioned or "out of it."

She might even hurt your feelings by making fun not only of your viewpoints but of *you*! It's quite common for young teens to go to great lengths *not* to be seen with a parent, as if the parent is some kind of alien. Whereas your adolescent might have cherished those weekend afternoons or evenings with mom or dad at the movies, now she's likely not to want to be caught dead with you anywhere nearby! She might ask you to drop her off two blocks from her school so that her friends won't see that a parent has brought her to school. She may even go so far as to try to walk several steps ahead or behind you when the two of you go out somewhere, as if being seen with you will bring total humiliation.

As a parent, you'll quickly sense the changes brought about by the influence of your teen's friends. Because of her strong desire to fit in with her peers, she's likely to copy many of their behaviors.

She may try to dress to fit in with a certain group norm, to begin using slang or other verbal expressions reflecting the "in" language of her agemates, and will probably be quick to point out the privileges her friends are allowed that she is denied. She's likely to show passionate loyalty to specific friends, becoming very defensive if you question or criticize their behavior.

Needless to say, such a change in your teenager is bound to create clashes with you. One of your biggest challenges becomes finding ways to influence your teen without putting down her peers and alienating her further.

COMMON DILEMMAS

"INAPPROPRIATE" FRIENDS

You're getting concerned about fourteen-year-old Brian's choice of friends. He's starting to hang around with a group of kids who look rebellious in the way they dress, and some of them are a couple of years older than your son. The school counselor has admitted that the peers Brian is choosing for friends are considered to be troublemakers.

Most parents tend to think of kids who dress in a certain manner, make poor grades, and are not heavily involved in extracurricular school activities as a potential "bad influence" on their teen. Parents, of course, can be wrong! Sometimes they become blinded by their own prejudices and jump to hasty conclusions.

A parent might read "disrespect" or "rebellion" into a style of dress or haircut that is just a fad or simply represents a teen's quest to be an individual. Certainly not every long-haired kid with an earring is a drug addict! And not every teenager who dresses to conform to a particular peer group will copy *every* aspect of that group's behavior. For example, your teen might have a friend who shoplifts, but he would not shoplift himself. Whether or not an adolescent is easily influenced to copy a peer's behavior very much depends upon that youngster's personality.

Sometimes school personnel will validate a parent's "sixth sense" by subtly or directly telling the parent to try to steer the teen away from a particular teen or group. This gives the parent's concern a little more substance, since the school staff has the advantage of being able to compare a teen's behavior against the norm for the larger peer community.

While you might be correct about your assumptions that certain of your teen's friends are rebels, abuse alcohol or drugs, are involved in a gang, or are unmotivated toward positive goals, the problem is that your adolescent will not consider your suspicions or facts to be any reason for him to discontinue a friendship with a particular teen or peer group.

Teens will typically attack your views as irrational and highly prejudiced, throwing the "you can't judge a book by its cover" theory right back in your face. They will point out, sometimes correctly, that you have jumped to conclusions based on rumors and appearances. To make matters even more complicated, your teen might sometimes involve himself with a peer group in which one or two youngsters are a little "iffy" but the rest are basically okay kids.

If you cite negative facts about a particular peer (such as prior school suspensions, arrests, and so on), your teenager is likely to defend the peer by saying that his friend was misunderstood or has changed for the better. In any case, you will usually not be able to convince your adolescent about the accuracy of other adults' perceptions.

You can have more influence on your teen by having a matter-of-fact (nonhysterical) conversation about the kind of trouble adolescents can unwittingly get into when they hang out with kids who engage in illegal or dangerous activities. For example, you could point out that if the police break up a party where teens are drinking alcohol, all of the youngsters are likely to get into trouble, even one who's not drinking. This type of rational discussion can certainly have an impact on some teens.

Generally speaking, however, forbidding a friendship with a particular peer not only won't work, it may also strengthen the bond between the two friends and/or increase the teen's rebellion toward a parent. This is especially true when the two peers go to school together, as there's nothing a parent can do to prevent their interacting while they're at school.

What does work is for you to establish rules for your teen about where, and under what circumstances, he's allowed to go out as well as the time he is to be home. If your teen breaks a rule, he pays the consequence with some form of restriction or grounding. If he's in the company of the "undesirable" peer when he gets in trouble, you can restrict the two adolescents from being together for a period of time, even lasting beyond the restriction. In other words, if your teen sneaks out of the house at night with Johnny, you might ground him for two weeks for sneaking out, and restrict him for an additional two weeks from spending time with Johnny.

This tactic is based on the teen's having gotten into trouble rather than on speculation about the motivations or character of the friend. It also serves another purpose. Peers who are rebellious and/or unsupervised by their parents will usually not stay around a teen who is still under parental control, preferring to seek the company of other peers who do not have to account for their whereabouts. In the long run, the "undesirable" peer will drop your teen because he's just not much fun if he has to obey rules. Likewise, an older teen is not going to want to hang out with a younger one who has to follow rules that are appropriate for the younger age group.

In spite of the problems mentioned, some parents will still insist that they want to forbid any contact between their teenager and one or more "undesirable" peers. These parents will often say that they don't care how much their teen might dislike them for this maneuver or how rebellious the teen might feel; they are willing to risk these negative repercussions.

Whether or not this plan will work depends on the level of rebellion of the teenager and, more important, on how tightly the parents can monitor their teen's out-of-school time. It is rare for most parents to be able to supervise a teen at all times, but some are able to take the teen to work with them or to have the youngster stay with a willing relative during the time the parent cannot be at home. The younger teen who is still more dependent on a parent might begrudgingly accept this plan; an older teen, however, might escalate the situation by leaving home.

Sometimes parents will try to combat the undesirable-friends phenomenon by moving their adolescent to a different school. The problem with this plan (which often doesn't work) is that it doesn't address the underlying issue of *why* the teen is seeking out an undesirable peer group in the first place. As much as you might hate to admit it, kids seek out their particular group of friends for a reason. That's why knowing who your teen's friends are can tell you a lot about your own adolescent. It's much more important to look at what's going on with your own teen rather than blaming his undesirable behavior on his peers.

Moving an adolescent to a new school can be an effective solution *if* he has truly changed his attitude toward the "undesirable" peers. For example, a teen who has gotten into trouble with a particular group of peers and then genuinely decides to seek out a new group of "straight" friends might well benefit from changing schools. But if he is forced against his will to switch to a new school to get away from a particular peer group, chances are he'll seek out the same kind of friends in the new school.

THE PHONE

Thirteen-year-old Jenny is constantly talking on the phone or e-mailing her friends over the Internet. She used to talk a lot to you, and you're feeling a little rejected. You're glad she has friends, but you'd prefer that she spend more time with the family.

The telephone and the Internet play an important role in your teen's becoming independent. Whereas she used to confide primarily in her parents, now she needs to begin the process of emotional separation from them. Although you might feel uncomfortable about it, it's developmentally appropriate for her to turn more and more to her own age group for support and advice.

It's not uncommon for a teen to come home from having spent several hours with her friends and immediately call or e-mail each one as quickly as she can get to it. Strange as it might seem to you, she's really engaging in much more than idle chitchat. What she's doing is getting reassurance about all those insecurities that come with being a teenager. If you restrict her phone or Internet use too severely, you'll be denying her this healthy opportunity.

If you're wondering *But why isn't she talking more to me?* realize that it's no longer appropriate for her to tell you *everything* about her life. This doesn't mean that she no longer needs you, because she does. She still needs your love, guidance, emotional support, and willingness to set limits if she gets out of line. She'll still want to confide in you at times, but probably *after* she's talked things over with her friends. And there will be some issues she'll want to tell you that she won't want her friends to know about, and vice versa.

Rather than seeing your teen's phone or Internet use as a rejection of you, look at it as a positive step in her becoming independent. You can take pleasure in watching her reach out to others and in knowing that she's not isolating herself from her peers.

On the other hand, a teen's use of the phone or Internet is a privilege that carries with it certain responsibilities: both must be used with appropriate limits.

For the phone, that means not making prank calls or unapproved long-distance calls, remembering to consider the right of other family members to have access to the phone, and respecting the family's need to not be unnecessarily disrupted by a ringing phone.

If you are a parent who gets or makes frequent phone calls in the evenings for social or work purposes, you'll not want your teen to occupy your line for long periods of time. One solution to this dilemma is to get a "teen" phone line, perhaps making it possible for your adolescent to earn the money for it. This option has the obvious advantage of allowing you to ignore any incoming calls for your teen if she isn't at home, and saves you the hassle of becoming a message center. It also provides wonderful leverage, since you can remove the phone by unhooking it from the jack for disciplinary purposes!

Another option is to set a time limit on your teen's use of the phone. This can be done per phone call (so many minutes per call, so many calls per night), or by designating certain time slots for her phone use (for example, from 5:00 until 6:00 P.M., and 7:30 until 8:30 P.M. each day). If you have two or more teens who argue about using the phone, you might designate time slots for each one (one gets the even hours, the other gets the odd hours).

Whatever your system, you'll probably want to set a phone dead-line each evening, earlier for school nights and later for non-school nights.

If you don't care how long your teen talks on the phone so long as you have ready access for your own calls, you might consider getting the Call Waiting feature. If a call comes in for you (or your mate), the teen agrees to give up her call until you are finished with yours.

At those times when your teenager is on the phone and you want to use it, remember to make a request rather than to issue a demand. You might say something like, "Honey, I understand that you need to talk to your friend, but I'm expecting a call in a few minutes. Will you please get off the phone until I get that call?" This request acknowledges your understanding that your teen's call is important to her, but lets her know that the phone is not for her use alone.

If your adolescent violates the agreed-upon phone rules, the simplest (and very effective!) method of solving the problem is to take her phone privileges away for away for a period of time. Phone restriction can be for twenty-four hours, or up to a week or two, depending on the severity of the violation. If your teen makes unauthorized long-distance calls, insist that she pay the bill, either by using her allowance or by earning the money. If you have a "teen line," you can ask the phone company to disallow long-distance calls from that line if such calls become a problem.

Remember to give your youngster the same courtesy you'd expect yourself when you are on the phone. While you might be tempted to listen in on your teen's conversations, this is a serious violation of personal privacy. Just like everyone else, teens will rightfully become furious if they find out someone has been eaves-dropping on their conversations. Because this breach of trust can be very difficult to mend, it would be appropriate for you to break this rule *only* if you have serious reasons to suspect that your teen is involved in illegal activity.

Be sure to consult your teenager for ideas about how to solve your family's particular phone problems. She's apt to be much more cooperative if you consider her suggestions for setting up the rules (time limits on school and non-school nights, a reasonable schedule for her own and her siblings' phone use, etc.)

Rules for the Internet may include not logging on to unapproved chat rooms or Web sites and not corresponding with strangers without parental permission. Both require monitoring—check your search engine under "parental control" for resources about software that will do this for you. Be aware that teens can use the "Instant Message" feature to talk online with anyone at any time both are signed on, so you'll want to know who is listed in your child's "buddy list."

Many parents don't realize that teens can easily sign up for multiple free e-mail accounts (even creating different passwords!) other than ones parents have approved. The fact is that most teens are much more savvy about all aspects of the Internet than their parents, and can find ways to go around parental restrictions (especially on a friend's computer). Consequently, it becomes the job of parents to educate their teens on safe use of the Internet.

Obviously, teens must also consider the needs of other family members for time on the computer. Ground rules need to be set for both the computer and the phone if your household is to run smoothly. A little creativity blended with lots of cooperation is an ideal formula.

EMBARRASSMENT ABOUT PARENTS

You're driving fourteen-year-old Jared to school and notice that he becomes nervous as you get near the school grounds, looking to see if anyone he knows is in sight. He asks you to drop him off several blocks from his destination because it's just "too embarrassing" to be seen riding in your "tacky" car!

Adolescents can be most adept at finding *something* about their parents that humiliates them. Often it's a parent's appearance: hair-style, weight, age, style of dress, and so on. Sometimes it's a parent's behavior: too silly, too serious, and so on. And it can also be a parent's vehicle.

It's as though the teen, trying to find an independent identity for himself, has to go out of his way to reject whatever image his parent projects. Notice how adults will attempt to compliment a teenager by remarking "You're just like your dad" or "You look just like your mother," only to have the teen roll his eyes as if he's just been given the biggest insult on the planet!

Even though you might be aware of this common adolescent phenomenon, it can still be difficult to hear that your own flesh and blood prefers not to be seen in public with you. If your teen rejects you for something that *you* yourself feel bad about, you will probably end up with hurt feelings. It will be much easier to toss off his remarks if you feel that there's no validity to them. In the example above, if you feel embarrassed to drive the car you own, you'll have a more difficult time with your teen's request to drop him off several blocks from the school than if you like your vehicle and can smile to yourself about your son's immaturity. So it's important to know what part of your hurt is your *own* issue so that you don't place all the blame on your teen.

The way you respond to these kinds of disparaging remarks from your teenager should depend less on *what* he says than on *how* he says them. It's one thing for him to ask you to drop him off three blocks from school as a polite request, possibly with an apologetic tone. In this case, you could tease him about his sensitivity, perhaps joking him about his lack of appreciation for your car's many marvelous qualities, and drop him off at the place he requested. Or if he's making fun of something about your appearance, you could say, "Well, I know I'm not Mrs. America (or some popular teen idol), but I'm not exactly chopped liver either!"

It's quite another matter if your teen is rude or insulting when he tells you that he is embarrassed to be seen with you, or if he orders you to do something out of the ordinary (dropping him off where friends can't see you, or refusing to walk beside you because of something about your appearance). In this case, refuse the request and tell him that you feel angry and/or hurt by his behavior. If it's not appropriate to talk at that time, save further discussion about the incident until later.

When you do have time to explore the matter, let your teen know that his rudeness and demeanor were inappropriate. Ask him if he's angry with you about something and, if he is, encourage him to air his grievance with you. Be sure to let him know that such remarks and/or behavior as he displayed can hurt people's feelings, and that parents are people too!

What if your teen sincerely insists that he is mortified about being seen in your car or about some aspect of your appearance or behavior? This can be a good opportunity to discuss values and priorities. Perhaps you aren't thrilled with your car, either, but don't have a newer one because you are saving money for your teen's education, or because you are trying to get out of debt. Maybe you need to remind him that standards about what's "in" in hairstyles, clothing, cars, and so on are fads. In contrast, what's really important is that a person likes *who he is* and *what he stands for*, and feels comfortable with his own appearance, actions, and choices. Rather than simply chewing him out about his rudeness, calmly let him know why such remarks represent a superficial point of view.

PEER PRESSURE ABOUT CLOTHES

Sixteen-year-old David is grumbling because he has "nothing to wear." When you remind him of his closet full of clothes, he informs you that his friends make fun of his wardrobe because he doesn't wear the more popular "designer" brands.

Rather than launching into a lecture about the evils of materialism, try to be sympathetic to what your son is experiencing. Teenagers have always had fads in clothing, hairstyles, and accessories. Whether it's thick bobby socks, crinolines, ankle bracelets, peace-sign jewelry, Bermuda shorts, long hair, baggy clothes, Mohawks, multiple earrings on one ear, black lipstick, purple hair, rock-band T-shirts, nose rings, or whatever, you can probably remember how important it was to own the "in" things to wear when your generation was in high school.

Instead of telling your teenager that he *shouldn't* want what he wants, try using a technique called *granting the wish in fantasy*. For example, you might say something like "Honey, I wish I could not only buy you that (designer) shirt, but I wish I could get you one in every color they make. It's just that it's not in the budget!"

or, "David, I'd love it if I could give you a thousand dolars to go buy yourself an entire designer wardrobe. But you know that your dad had to take a cut in pay, and money is really tight right now." This tactic, *if not used sarcastically*, makes your teen feel that you are his ally rather than his enemy, but makes it clear that you are not going to buy the desired item.

It's also wise to try to help your teenager think of a way he *might* be able to purchase some prized item that is important to him. For instance, if you usually buy him four pairs of nondesigner jeans, you could offer him the choice of using the same money for two pairs of designer jeans (and perhaps doing his laundry more frequently). You could also offer to contribute the amount of money you plan to spend for a pair of regular jeans, and let him pay for or earn the *difference* in price so that he can buy the designer pair.

You might wonder if this approach doesn't encourage a materialistic attitude toward life that may conflict with your own value system. Certainly, you'll make the point with your teen that preoccupation with how much money one spends on clothes and other items is a superficial stance and that a person's character or value is not measured by the expense of the items that person possesses. But allowing him to have the *option* of owning an expensive item by giving up something for it, or by earning it, encourages the realistic view that one makes choices and sets priorities in life. It may be that by getting the "designer" item under these circumstances, he'll learn that it really would have been much more practical and convenient to have forfeited the expensive jeans.

Parents teach adolescents to be materialistic not by offering them realistic options but by granting their every wish and buying them anything and everything the parents can afford. Allowing a teen to make choices and sacrifices in order to get something he dearly desires allows him to learn what is valuable via his own experience. This stance also lets a parent remain supportive and encouraging with a teen rather than becoming the "heavy" who tells him he shouldn't want what he wants.

COPYCAT

Thirteen-year-old Janie has suddenly begun to change her style of clothing, her hairstyle, her walk, and even the way she talks. It's not that there's anything offensive about any of these changes. What bothers you is that she is meticulously copying the dress, mannerisms, and language of her new group of friends, and you worry that she'll lose her own identity in the process.

There's no reason to panic at this point. Teens desperately want to fit in with their peers, and often try to accomplish this by copying to a *T* the group to which they want to belong. So long as what they're copying isn't problematic, you can chalk this up to typical early adolescent behavior. As they mature, teens will generally become freer to deviate from their own select group and to express more of their own uniqueness.

This copying process is actually a step in a teen's identity formation. It's like trying on a new role, seeing how it fits, and then trying on another for a while. The more insecure the teen, the more likely she'll be to jump into a totally new role in order to feel that she belongs. Gradually she'll keep what fits her personality, casting the rest aside.

But what if your teen is copying negative behavior, or offensive language or clothing? What if she's trying to fit in with a group that goes against your own moral values (becoming a skinhead, dressing seductively, using obscene words, and so on)? What if she sneaks certain unacceptable clothing to school, changing clothes after she leaves home? If this happens with your teen, tell her that such behavior is unacceptable and that you will not allow it. Set a firm limit as soon as you notice the problem and explain why you feel the way you do. Consider confiscating items of clothing that she's "sneaked," telling her that she can have them back once you're reassured that she will not wear them to school. Remember, you're goal is not to win a popularity contest with your teen but to stand the heat when you're sticking up for your principles.

REJECTED BY A FRIEND

Fourteen-year-old Sandy is devastated because her childhood best friend seems to be ignoring her and hanging out with another girl.

Friendships are so important in adolescence that it can be very traumatic for a teen to be rejected by someone she regards as a friend. It can be especially upsetting if she feels betrayed by a "best friend."

Of course, as a parent, you have no control over this situation. It wouldn't be wise to call up the "best friend" (or her parents) and try to patch things up (even if you could), as your daughter would be likely to feel humiliated and upset with you for meddling. So how can you help her through this difficult time?

Let your teen know that you unserstand what she's going through. Many parents, in an effort to be helpful, try to minimize the adolescent's pain by reminding her that she has other friends and/or by recounting all the negative things about the friend's character and behavior. The "you're better off without her, anyway" approach may be accurate, but it is likely to result in your teen's perceiving you as "not understanding." Realize that she *is* experiencing a loss and that it's appropriate and normal for her to grieve about it.

Ask your daughter to tell you why she thinks the other girl might want to end their friendship. Have they been having arguments lately? Did she do something that may have hurt the friend's feelings? Is the other girl jealous of your daughter for some reason? Is it that the two have been growing apart due to different interests as they mature? This discussion should help your teen put the matter in perspective, at least helping her explain things to herself even though she'll still have to deal with her feelings of anger or sadness.

If she hasn't already done so, encourage your teen to talk with her friend to try to resolve whatever is causing the problem. One doesn't just walk away from a good friendship without first trying to heal the rift. Suggest that she ask the other girl to talk over the situation, saying something like "I've noticed that we haven't talked much lately, and I wonder if something's wrong or if I've done something that upset you. We've been such good friends, can't we get together and talk this out?" She could make this request in person, by giving the friend a note, or by calling on the phone, whichever is most comfortable for her.

By suggesting this action, you are teaching your teen an important lesson about the value of friendship and emotional intimacy. People do have misunderstandings and conflicts. By confronting a friend and trying to reconcile the problem, the friendship is often strengthened. If the friend is uncooperative or insists on ending the friendship, at least the person trying to resolve the issue can feel good about making the effort to preserve the relationship. So point out to your teen that you are proud of her for having the courage to pursue healing the relationship with her friend, even if her efforts fail.

Unless your teen and her ex-friend become close again, realize that it will probably take some time before your teen will be at peace over the loss. In the meantime, you'll certainly want to encourage her to actively seek out new friends (for ideas on this, see the discussion under the next topic).

NOT HAVING FRIENDS

Sixteen-year-old Jim seems to get along with his peers in school, yet he remains a loner. He doesn't go out with friends on the weekends and rarely receives phone calls.

While many perfectly well-adjusted teens do not run with the "popular" crowd or have a swarm of friends, most do have at least one or two good friends of the same sex with whom they hang out. When this doesn't occur, it's natural for a parent to become concerned.

Let's assume at this point that your teen's not having friends is *not* due to depression or some other emotional problem (for a discussion of these issues, see Chapter Nine). In other words, he seems to you to be a normal teenager in every other way. He's doing reasonably well academically, he has some interests besides watching television, he seems to be in a good mood most of the time, and he is not embroiled in a serious family conflict.

First, you'll want to determine whether your son is just naturally shy or if he's doing something to alienate his peers. If you're not sure about this, you might want to check with a few of his teachers at school or perhaps the school counselor to see if they can shed any light on the issue. There's also the possibility that he is rejecting his peers because of *their* behavior (they are snobbish, they abuse alcohol or drugs, and so on). Perhaps he's decided not to try to have friends because of an earlier painful experience with a peer.

WHEN YOUR TEEN IS ALIENATING OTHERS

Common ways that your teen might be contributing to his own social problems with his peers include putting down other people, acting like a know-it-all, having a chip-on-the-shoulder attitude, having an expolsive temper, seeming like a goodie-goodie, being bossy, lying, or bragging. If your adolescent is doing one or more of these things, you'll obviously want to tell him specifically how you think he may be responsible for alienating his peers.

Of course, almost nobody likes to be told about his faults, and adolescents are often even more defensive about them. The most constructive and sensitively delivered criticism will often fall on disgruntled ears. So be prepared for your teen to reject your perception of his difficulty. Some teens, however, will take your message to heart and may decide to change their behavior as a result of your feedback. This is more likely to occur if you calmly and matter-of-factly point out your teen's alienating behavior only after first giving him feedback about his *positive* qualities.

If you find your teen unwilling to admit his responsibilty for alienating peers (if that's what's happening), there's still another option available to you. Check with your teen's school counselor to see if the school offers groups for improving peer relationships, or with a community agency or private mental health professional who offers group therapy for adolescents. Confrontation with one's peers is generally the most effective way to get a teen to change his style of relating, and such groups, assisted by a facilitator or psychotherapist, provide this opportunity.

If your teen is unreceptive to participating in such a group, negotiate with him to go for a trial month to check it out. If he's still unreceptive at the end of the month, let him know that you'll not insist he continue (since he's unlikely to get much out of it anyway if he doesn't like it).

If the teen-group approach doesn't work, or if you cannot find such a group in your community, seek a consultation with a mental health professional who works with adolescents.

WHEN YOUR TEEN IS SHY OR IS RELUCTANT TO MAKE FRIENDS

If your adolescent is friendless due to his being shy, is rejecting peers because he disapproves of their behavior, or is afraid to be hurt by friends because of a past experience, he obviously needs to learn to make friends with whom he'll feel compatible. One of the best and easiest ways for him to find such friends is to participate in a sport he likes or to join a club or group. Whether it's a karate class, a racquetball league, a chess club, a drama group, or a church/synagogue youth organization, joining some formal group allows your teen to meet a different group of peers from those with whom he associates on an individual basis. Even if the team or organization is a school activity involving peers with whom he's already acquainted, he's likely to get to know them— and them to know him—in a different way.

Of course, many times the solution to your teen's making new friends lies in his joining groups that aren't associated with his school. Such classes and organizations provide a while new set of peers, ones that share some common interest. By being involved in an activity or in planning some project of mutual interest, the shy teen doesn't have to work so hard to think of conversation. Even if he makes just one friend out of the group, his participation will be well worth it.

If your teen is reluctant or unwilling to join extracurricular activities or groups, you might have to make his participation mandatory in order for him to enjoy certain privileges he wants or takes for granted (taking Driver's Education, driving the car, having his own phone, getting an increase in allowance, and so on). Many parents find it helpful to require a teen to participate in a minimum of one or two extracurricular activities a week, but leave the *choice* of the activity up to the teen. It needs to be made clear, however, that the chosen activity requires active participation (unlike some high school clubs where a student can remain a passive participant and attend meetings once a month).

If a suitable group or activity is unavailable, or if your teen is balking and maintaining that nothing interests him, suggest an alternative: He can do volunteer work for a specified number of hours per week. Some adolescents really like this idea. Others will suddenly manage to find a sport, club, or activity that they can tolerate!

Also be sure that your adolescent knows *how* to make friends. As strange as this might seem, many teens act as if they expect friends to drop from the sky, without any effort on their part. You'll need to convince your teen to become proactive about making friends. Suggest that he greet his peers by saying "hello" (preferably adding their name) rather than remaining silent when he sees them, and that he initiate simple conversation with appropriate questions (What do you think of that assignment she gave us in biology?" "How did our swim team do in yesterday's meet?" "What have you picked for your English project?"). Encourage him to notice something unusual about a peer and ask about it ("You look bummed out today. Is something wrong?" "Looks like you got some new boots!").

Remember to encourage your adolescent to invite friends to your house at appropriate times. Find out if there's something about your house or about your family that makes him uncomfortable or embarrassed to have them over. If he mentions an issue to you, matter-of-factly problem-solve about the solution rather than becoming defensive or accusatory.

SNEAKING OUT AT NIGHT

You've just discovered that fourteen-year-old Misty has been sneaking out of the house at night. When you confront her, she

*tells you that "everybody does it," making it sound as if you are
being unreasonable for being upset with her behavior.*

Although you'll certainly want to set a serious consequence
for your daughter's sneaking out at night, know that such behavior is quite typical for many adolescents. In many communities,
there is a great deal of peer pressure to "sneak out," and kids who
don't are often made fun of by their peers. Teens find this behavior a thrill because they are flouting the rules set by adults regarding staying up late, being in a group without adult supervision,
and doing as they please. So your teen's participation is not the
end of the world, or a sign that she has some terrible character
problem.

Obviously, you'll want to find out where your teen went and
what she did when she left home in this manner. You'll probably
feel a little relieved if she's been engaging in innocent mischief. If
she's been involved in a situation where sex, drugs, and/or alcohol were part of the scene, naturally your concern will be intensi-
fied, and the situation might even require evaluation by a mental
health professional (see chapters 7 and 9 for suggestions on how
to deal with these important issues).

Of course, you'll feel furious, perhaps scared, about your
adolescent's violation of your trust. No matter how innocent her
behavior or intentions, it is the trust issue that must be stressed
with her. Let her understand that once a breach of trust has
occured, it doesn't get healed overnight. No matter how remorseful she might be or how many promises she might make about
her never repeating this behavior, only the passage of time (probably many months) will restore your trust that she won't sneak
out at night again. Warn her in advance that she will undoubt-
edly feel furious with you in the near future when, even though
she may be telling you the truth, you'll be unable to respond with
total confidence, no matter how much you love her and *want* to
be able to trust her.

Be glad that you've discovered your teen's sneaking out, as
this behavior will typically continue until an adolescent is caught.
Give her a restriction lasting several weeks, the duration depending on the seriousness of her activities during her time away from

home. Remember to provide an opportunity for her to earn back *some* privilege every week or two of her restriction so that she doesn't feel overwhelmed by the enormity of the consequence.

While you don't want to be pessimistic and suspicious about your daughter's having learned her lesson, you also don't want to be naive. Consider randomly setting your alarm for an early morning hour for a while, especially on weekends, and just check to see who's in bed. You don't have to announce this to your teen, and she'll probably be unaware of it unless she's caught sneaking out again. Obviously, a second infraction would result in a more serious penalty, and if this behavior continues, a consultation with a mental health professional would be recommended.

THE BOY WHO'S NOT "MACHO"

Sixteen-year-old Chad is constantly teased by other boys for not being "macho." In his community, most of the teenage boys like to hunt, drink beer, and brag about their sexual exploits. Chad simply doesn't share these interests, and his male peers see him as a wimp.

Whenever a teen has interests or values that are different from those of the majority of his peers, he's likely to face teasing, ridicule, or rejection. The most effective way to help your teen deal with such discrimination is to encourage him to find emotional support via a *different* peer group. If he can't find a couple of friends who support his own views, he may need to look outside of his own high school.

Encourage your teen to join groups or organizations that are likely to have beliefs similar to his own. In this case, he might find an environmental group, a human rights organization, or a group that revolves around one of his hobbies or interests. Through contact with such a group, he's likely to make some new friends.

As for his dealing with his schoolmates, encourage him to have a lighthearted, casual response to their teasing. If he becomes indignant, insulted, or self-righteously superior, he's only likely to spur his critics to further attack. He might say something like

"Come on, guys, give me a break!" or "Sorry, that's just not my thing!' or "Okay! So I'm weird!" If he can manage this kind of response *without any signs of emotional distress*, the teasers are more likely to leave him alone.

You'll also want to let your teen know that part of growing up involves learning how to stand up for one's own beliefs, unpopular though they might be. Let him know that you see strength in his not capitulating to his peers just to win popularity.

In the case of a boy who's being teased about not being macho, it certainly helps to have an adult male he respects who models the nonmacho version of masculinity. It's fine for him to hear that he's "man enough" from a woman, but it's more important that he receive validation of his masculinity from a man.

JEALOUSY

Seventeen-year-old Anne is becoming very irritable lately. You think it's because she's jealous that her best friend is getting a new car for her approaching high-school graduation.

Let's face it. It's hard, even as mature adults, not to become a bit envious of the good fortune of our friends if we feel that our own lives are difficult by comparison, or if we think that we are more deserving than the person who is getting the goodies.

Teenagers, without the benefit of maturity, can have a very hard time if they feel they've been dealt an unfair deal. Things like having an affluent lifestyle, having romance in one's life, and being highly attractive are many teens' idea of heaven on earth. A friend's good fortune can be hard to swallow if you don't have some of the same benefits.

To help your teen deal with jealousy, she'll first need to acknowledge that she feels it. Rather than an insensitive "I just think you're upset because you're jealous of Elizabeth," try a little more indirect approach. Ask your teen if she realizes she's been acting irritated a lot lately and that you're wondering if something is bothering her. If she doesn't convince you that there's another reason for her behavior and doesn't mention the jealousy issue, offer your interpretation. You might say something like "Well, I don't know if this is true for you, but *I* would really be a little jealous of someone's getting a fantastic car for graduation, especially if I didn't even own a car. Do you think this could be bugging you?"

Whether your daughter agrees or denies that she feels jealous, you can go on to talk about the dynamics of jealousy. Let her know that such feelings are (would be) perfectly normal, and don't mean that she isn't (wouldn't be) really happy for Elizabeth. It just means (would mean) that she'd like to have some of the same experiences Elizabeth is having.

It's important to stress to adolescents that life truly isn't fair and that those who expect it to be so are in for a rude awakening. The fact is that some teens have families who can give them more material advantages. The person who works the hardest or follows the rules doesn't necessarily get the rewards. There is satisfaction in having personal integrity, however, and in doing a job well.

It can also help to point out to your adolescent that many people who have every financial and material advantage are unhappy or troubled. This may or may not be true for her friend, but the point is that money (or attractiveness) do not *guarantee* a person's happiness. For every person, there will always be *someone* who has more money, *someone* who is considered to be more attractive, and *someone* who is blessed with a bigger stroke of good luck.

Encourage your teenager to focus on her own strengths and to set realistic goals for herself. If she's upset because she's wishing she could buy a car, explore ways she might work toward that goal. In other words, help your teen specify a goal, identify the resources she'll need to attain it, and make specific plans to identify and take that first step toward its accomplishment.

SELECTING ONE FRIEND OVER ANOTHER

Eighteen-year-old Kelly is in a quandary. She has two good friends who each want her to room with them in the college dorm. She does have a preference, but is afraid of hurting the other girl's feelings.

Certainly you'll sympathize with your daughter's plight, and you can also compliment her on her sensitivity to other people's feelings. You'll need to let her know, however, that rejection in a personal context always leads to some hurt feelings. Consequently, it's impossible to say or do some magic thing that will prevent her friend from feeling *some* hurt when she tells her that she's going to room with the other girl.

At the same time, life involves making choices, and part of maturing is to confront those choices rather than run away from them. So she'll need to level with her friend about whom she prefers to be her roommate, and to do it as quickly as possible (so that the other girl can make other plans).

Obviously, the way she tells her friend about her decision can make a difference in the degree of hurt that friend will feel and can also affect their future relationship. So help your daughter formulate her response so that she is clear, truthful, and will, hopefully, preserve the friendship.

Suggest that your teen begin the conversation by telling her friend that this decision about roommates has been very difficult because she truly cares a great deal about both friends and does not want to hurt either of their feelings. However, she's decided to room with the other girl because she feels the two of them are more compatible as *roommates*, which is different from being compatible as friends who don't live together. It would be helpful to give some examples of potential incompatibility at this point: "You like to stay up very late and I like to go to bed early," "You're a neatnik and I'm a slob," "I like my space and to go places alone, and you're more of a people person."

She should reassure her friend that she still wants to spend time with her and to stay close. She might also add a statement like "Because you are such a good friend, I knew you would understand my decision, and that you would know better than to think we still can't be best friends."

Helping your teen work through this difficult situation will give her a valuable lesson in communication that she can apply to any emotionally intimate relationship. Congratulate yourself on getting this opportunity by being a parent whom she can confide in and one whose opinion she obviously respects.

FIVE

HOUSE RULES

One of the first ways a teenager will test her independence is to challenge the rules at home. She might actively protest that they are unreasonable, or she might just quietly rebel and simply not follow them. Typically, hassles occur around issues of responsibility, the teen's pressure to have more personal freedom, and the adolescent's disagreement with a parent's preferences.

She might argue about the fairness of having to do specific chores, especially cleaning her room. She might crusade for a later bedtime, a raise in allowance, or the privilege of having friends at home when a parent isn't present. She might beg to paint her room black or to listen to music a parent considers inappropriate. She might balk at going to church or synagogue, or even at having to eat meals with the family. She could even argue for permission to do something that is illegal, such as driving the family car before she has a learner's permit or driver's license.

Not only will adolescents begin to challenge the rules, but they are also likely to become highly critical of their parents and to try to manipulate the grown-ups against one another. They'll seek out the most liberal, permissive, or inconsistent parent in an effort to get what they want. When parents polarize into "good guy" and "bad guy" roles, the resulting conflict can cause serious marital problems and greatly increase family tensions.

A parent's toughest job is to set reasonable limits that are consistent with a teen's level of maturity. The problem is that teens often think they are more mature than they are and resent being treated "like a baby." Some parents, of course, have a hard time easing up on parental control and allowing adolescents to show that they *are* ready for more freedom. The process often becomes one of a parent's ambivalently granting a teen a new privilege and, if the adolescent behaves inappropriately, having to rescind it. As you can imagine, a parent who must insist on reducing a teen's freedom will not receive much gratitude from the teen, making it all the more difficult for a parent who shies away from conflict.

Since a teenager is usually only one member of the household, rules must be negotiated that take everyone's feelings and needs into consideration. Flexibility without compromising safety, as always, is the key to having house rules that everyone in the family can live with comfortably.

COMMON DILEMMAS

"I NEED MY SPACE!"

When thirteen-year-old Blaire arrives home from school, she heads straight to her room, shuts the door, and stays there most of the night. What happened to your formerly congenial kid who liked to hang out in the kitchen while you prepared dinner, and who loved to sit around with the rest of the family most of the evening?

As children turn into teenagers, they begin to want more privacy. They're beginning the process of separating emotionally from their parents, and that's a difficult thing to accomplish when they're hanging out in the center of family activity. They're also beginning the process of switching loyalty from their parents to their peers.

Much of the time when they're in their rooms (or any other

place where they're isolated from the rest of the family), teens are, if at all possible, on the phone with friends. When they can't be with friends, either in person on via the phone, they'll typically listen to music, watch television, introspect about themselves, fantasize, and review the events of the day. If parents are lucky, their teens might even be doing homework!

Since adolescents are bonding with their peers, they're unlikely to confide in their parents as often as they once did. Parents often become concerned that their teens are becoming secretive when, in fact, their adolescents are expressing a normal need for privacy. There's no reason for parents to feel hurt, rejected, unneeded, or that there's something wrong with their parenting because their teens "want some space."

But how are you to know if your teen is spending *too much* time in her room? When does an adolescent's normal need to be alone turn into emotional withdrawal, isolation, and possible depression? The best way to answer this question is to look at the bigger picture of your teen's overall adjustment. If she's doing reasonably well in school (or if she isn't, but she's trying to improve), has friends, is in a good or contented mood much of the time, and seems to look forward to *something* that's constructive, you probably don't have anything to worry about. If not, you'll want to explore the possibility that she is troubled or depressed (for a discussion of depression, see Chapter Nine).

While it's unrealistic to think that your teen will be thrilled to spend large amounts of time with the family, this doesn't mean that she shouldn't be expected to participate in some routine family activities. It's helpful, if at all possible, to insist that she eat the evening meal with the family during the week, as well as at least one weekend meal. If a commitment makes her late on occasion for the regular mealtime, there's no harm in letting her eat alone on those nights. But if she has such commitments most every school night, at least one parent might sit with her while she eats, providing an opportunity to catch up on what's happening in one another's lives.

But what about the teen who wants to skip a meal because she's not hungry, doesn't feel well, has too much homework, or is upset about something? If this request is an occasional thing, you can show respect for her feelings by allowing her to miss the meal. If she asks to skip a meal very often, let her know that you expect her to sit at the dinner table during the meal just to spend some time with the family, even if she doesn't eat. Obviously, this policy will be easier to enforce if you set it up early on.

It's also not unreasonable to insist that your teen participate in some weekly family experience beside meals. This could be a "family night" during the week where everyone gets together for a couple of hours to do some agreed-upon activity (go to a sports event, watch a special program or movie on television, make plans for an upcoming vacation, and so on). However, schoolwork often interferes with such plans, and it can be difficult to schedule around it if you have more than one child or teen.

Another possibility is to plan a weekend activity, usually for just a few hours. Teens are more likely to participate willingly in a family function if they know they won't be locked into a commitment that lasts most of the day. For a special occasion when the family will be involved in a whole day's event (going to a theme park, or driving out of town for some event or activity), give your adolescent the courtesy of letting him know about your plans well in advance. Teens really resent making plans with their friends on the weekend and then having to cancel them for a family activity.

If you're thinking of finding ways to increase your teen's participation in family functions, don't forget to ask her for her ideas. She's likely to be much more cooperative with the whole plan if her opinions and preferences are considered. You want your "family time" to be a win-win situation for everyone, or you'll defeat the whole purpose of having it.

Remember that just because your teen is in her room, it doesn't mean that you can't have some interaction with her. As long as you don't come across as nosy or as checking up on her (and she'll quickly figure out either, if that's what's happening), you can pop into her room (knocking first, to respect her privacy) for some friendly but brief interchange. And, much as she might protest that it's unnecessary or "stupid," stop by her room to tell her good night. If you do this with the right intent (not to harangue her about an issue), you might find that she'll open up and talk with you. These kinds of "spontaneous" talks are often the most enlightening and rewarding, strengthening the bond with your teen naturally and without effort.

CHORES

Sixteen-year-old Bret constantly has to be nagged to do the simplest chores around the house. Even when frequently reminded, he rarely does them without a battle. He even "forgets" to feed his own dog!

One of the biggest battles between parents and teens often occurs over household chores. Parents can become infuriated when they are working long hours and come home to find an adolescent lounging around after he's left a mess in the kitchen and done none of the tasks that he agreed to do.

Whether or not a parent works outside the home, or even if the family has a full-time housekeeper, it's important for kids of any age to have some responsibilities at home. The problem is that, in many households, the carrying out of chores is only a matter of lip service. Teens are given assigned duties and may be yelled at, threatened, or lectured when they don't comply. But the bottom line is they still get away with not having to fulfill their agreements, at least not until a parent blows up and issues an ultimatum. Instead of teaching adolescents to assume responsibility, parents are unwittingly giving them the message that procrastination, complaining, and rebelling will frequently pay off and get a person out of doing something he doesn't really want to do in the first place.

If your teenager is not one of the few who willingly performs his household duties, you might wonder how you can get him to do so without an all-out war. The secret lies in drawing up a clear contract with him about exactly *what* is to be done, and *when* it is to be done, rewarding compliance with *privileges* and noncompliance with specific *consequences*.

Obviously, the first step in this process is getting your teen's agreement that he will perform specific chores. Let him know that you are tired of all the hassle about chores and that you realize you only make him angry by nagging or yelling at him. Tell him you want to design a contract that spells out what each of you expects regarding chores and that you are willing to allow him certain privileges for his compliance.

Remember that privileges can be those "normal" pleasures he's already used to getting *but now has to earn*, or they can be something new that he hasn't yet experienced. Common privileges for teens include getting an allowance (or a raise in the amount), spending the night out, having a friend stay overnight, renting a video on the weekend, being allowed to have a television remain in his room the next week, going to a teen game parlor, or getting to drive the family car. When deciding upon specific privileges, you might even ask your teen, "What would it take to get you to do these three chores each week?" and see what he suggests. If his idea is outrageous, tell him, "Nice try! Now let's get realistic," and continue the negotiation.

Once you've explained the general idea to your adolescent, ask *him* to design a contract and present it to you. This rough draft would consist of his listing specific chores he's willing to do, and the privilege(s) he'd like to earn for doing them. Ask him when he can present this draft to you and your spouse and nail down a deadline that's not too far in the future. If the deadline occurs and he hasn't drafted the contract (and doesn't have a legitimate reason for not doing so), insist that you sit down with all concerned parties and draft it together. The point is that your adolescent will be much more likely to comply with an agreement if he's had an opportunity to participate actively in designing it. If he refuses, however, you'll have to initiate the process.

Once you've agreed on the chores and the privileges, the next step is to specify a *deadline* by which the weekly chores (cleaning room and/or bathroom, doing the laundry, vacuuming family room, etc.) must be done. Cooperation on daily chores (feeding the dog, unloading the dishwasher) can also be assessed at the time of the weekly deadline, as it is easier to have the "accounting" for the week's efforts occur at one specific time.

Many families prefer Thursday night as the weekly deadline,

perhaps at nine or ten o'clock. Teens like to know how much allowance they're getting and/or what privileges they will have for the weekend; parents like to know that their house is in order for the weekend.

The idea is that if the chores are done by the deadline, the teen earns the privilege. If they're not done, of course, the teen loses the privilege. But in addition, *all privileges stop* until the chores are completed. In other words, it's not a matter of the teen's deciding that he doesn't *have* to do the chore just because he's forfeited the privilege. The point is he loses the privilege and *all other* privileges until the chore is completed.

This means that he doesn't leave the house, except for a school or a school-related event, or some other formal commitment (participating in a sports team; a job), and that he doesn't have visitors, until he's fulfilled his obligation. Once your teen sees that you will hold him to the contract and that he can't get out of doing his chores, he will realize the benefits of performing his responsibilities in a timely manner.

Be sure to let your adolescent know that using this contract system will benefit him in several ways. He'll be able to keep or gain privileges that are important to him, and he will no longer have to put up with your nagging him to get things done. Most important, earning his privileges is now under *his* control rather than being dependent on *your* momentary mood. For example, if he's done his chores for the week but gets into an argument with you before school on Friday morning, you might become so angry with him that you impulsively ground him for part or all of the weekend. With the contract system, he'd already have earned his weekend privileges, so they wouldn't be subject to cancellation due to an emotional moment.

You, of course, also have benefits from using the contract approach. Obviously, you gain reassurance that your teen can no longer manipulate his way out of his household responsibilities. But you also get out of the position of being the "heavy." When he doesn't earn his maximum privileges, you are still in a position to remain his advocate. For example, you might say something like "I'm sorry you didn't get your top allowance this week; I know you were counting on buying that CD tomorrow. It seems that it's hard for you to remember to feed the cat in the morning. What do you think you could do next week to help yourself remember so that you can get that CD?"

The point is a contract for chores makes it clear that your teen gains or loses his privileges because of his own choices. No longer can he blame a parent for his mistakes.

CURFEWS

You're worried sick because seventeen-year-old Amy is an hour past the time she agreed to be home. She's driving the car, and you have fantasies of all kinds of awful things that might have happened to her. Then she walks in the door, sees that you're upset, looks at her watch, and says, "What's wrong? I'm not that late!"

Realize that teens are often astounded that their parents worry so much about them. They have that invulnerable feeling of youth that tells them "Nothing bad will happen to me!"

Given this mind-set, many teens see no good reason for even having a curfew, especially if they're juniors or seniors in high school. So curfews can become a real battleground as youngsters try to convince their skeptical parents that the parents are "babying" them by making them come home too early, or by setting any time limit at all.

Some teens, of course, will not need a time limit. They come home at a reasonable time and don't take advantage of not having a set curfew. Other adolescents will constantly test the limits, always pushing to stay out later than their parents think is reasonable. So it makes sense for parents to tie the presence or absence of a curfew—and the time limit allowed—to the teen's level of responsibility.

If your adolescent usually returns home when she promises, or calls you with a good reason if she is going to be late, there may be no need to raise the curfew issue. On the other hand, if she's unreliable about coming home at the time she agrees, or if she stays out later than you consider to be appropriate, you'll want to step in and set a specific time limit.

In the instance with Amy, you would probably feel quite angry at her for causing you such worry. Rather than launching into a speech about her irresponsibility, it would be best to give her the opportunity to explain why she was late. It's possible she has a very good reason and that your anger will vanish when you hear it. Although you've been frightened or angered, you still need to maintain your flexibility.

Even if her reason for being late is valid, it's likely that you'll still be irritated if she *could* have telephoned you but didn't. In this case, you'd discuss your expectation that she be more considerate in the future. Whether or not you give her some negative consequence (for her neglecting to call, for being late, or both) will depend on her history about such matters. If you simply decide that some ground rules are in order, plan to discuss them over the next couple of days when everyone involved is calm and clear-thinking rather than in the heat of the crisis.

When the time for discussion arrives, be sure to ask your teen for her input. Listen to her ideas about appropriate curfews, as well as telling her yours. Be sure to specify times to be home for both school and non–school nights.

If the two of you are negotiating a curfew and she wants a later time that you think is inappropriate, consider letting her "earn" the privilege of staying out half an hour or an hour later by meeting certain conditions over a specific time period. For example, if she does her chores without having to be reminded (or maintains a certain grade point average, or has no missing assignments) over the next six weeks, she'll begin the later curfew at that point. This system clearly links later curfews with a teen's demonstration of increased responsibility.

But what happens when she isn't home by the agreed-upon time? A system that makes sense, both to teens and to parents, is to allow a thirty-minute leeway. If a teen is *later* than thirty minutes, she must come in *one hour early* the next non–school night. If she's over thirty minutes late *two nights* in a row, she's grounded the *next* non–school night. Also, she must call home if she's going to be over the thirty-minute limit. If she doesn't, she loses the privilege of going out *two* non–school nights in a row.

Of course, everyone needs to realize that the thirty-minute lee-way is there to be used as a cushion. The adolescent who habitually appears twenty-nine minutes after the specified curfew is not abiding by the intent of the rule and might face having the curfew reset to thirty minutes earlier.

It should be clear that when your teen calls home to tell you she'll be late, the two of you will agree on the time for her to be home, depending on the situation that's causing the delay. This doesn't mean that she has carte blanche to stay out until the wee hours.

With this system, a teen clearly has a choice. If she just *has* to have a little extra time, she has up to the thirty-minute leeway without any penalty. If she chooses to go over that thirty-minute limit, she knows she's making the decision to come in an hour early on her next night out. On the other hand, she can't habitually come in over thirty minutes late or she'll lose an entire night out quite frequently.

Although this system works well for many families, you might not like the idea of giving a young teen a consistent time to be home. Instead, you'd prefer to set a curfew for each circumstance, gauging the time you want her home according to the activity she's planning on that particular outing. Older adolescents usually prefer to work with a set curfew, since they often don't know in advance exactly what they'll be doing or where they will be. Often, they gather at one friend's house, or at one meeting place, and then let their plans evolve spontaneously. Which system you use will depend on your own personal preferences and on what works best for your teen.

Sometimes conflicts occur about curfews because teens might want to stay out beyond the time the parent wants to go to bed. Of course, the parent wants to know what time the teen gets home, and to make sure that she returns in appropriate physical and emotional condition (not drunk, ill, stoned, injured, or emotionally upset).

A good solution to this dilemma is to have your teen awaken

you or your spouse upon returning home, thus establishing the time of arrival. On some of these occasions, it's wise for you to get up and briefly interact with your teen just to check out her condition. While she might accuse you of being silly and suspicious, she'll know deep inside that you are neither uncaring nor naive.

Of course, you might want to modify any system you've set up to better suit your own preferences. But whatever policy you set with your teen, make sure everyone understands exactly what the rules are, as well as the consequences for violating them. You might want to write the plan in the form of a contract so that everyone is clear about what was decided. But be sure to treat your teen as a person with some choices, rather than inviting her to feel like she's dangling from the end of a leash.

THE MESSY ROOM

Fifteen-year-old Lisa is driving you crazy because she will not keep her room tidy. Both clean and dirty clothes are strewn all over the floor and furniture, any flat surface is littered with miscellaneous papers, makeup, and jewelry, and you're terrified to look under her bed for fear of what might crawl out after you. Since you can't have the room condemned, what can you do?

One of the most infamous sources of conflict between parents and teens is "the room." Teenagers argue that it's *their* room, so they should be allowed to keep it in any condition they want. Parents retort that it is *their* house, so a teen's room should be kept to the household standard for cleanliness and neatness.

In addition to all the usual tactics parents resort to when they are in conflict with their teens, such as reasoning, lecturing, arguing, and yelling, some parents use the "wait it out" strategy for the problem room. The idea is that if they just wait long enough and don't say anything, their teenager's room will be such a source of embarrassment when her friends come over that she'll clean it up. Unfortunately, most teens have a maddening capacity to outlast the most patient parent, so this approach is usually doomed from the start. In fact, if you decide to try it, it's wise in advance to schedule an exterminator to come to your house in about six to eight weeks!

As a way out of this common dilemma, it helps to think in terms of whether or not the state of your teen's room realistically affects *you*, or other members of the household, in some *concrete* negative way (as opposed to affecting your thoughts or feelings about the matter). The "I just can't stand to look at it" doesn't count, because you *can* close her door, and the mess will not be seen by you or anyone else who doesn't choose to open the door and enter the room.

But what if you typically go into her room to collect her laundry? This concretely affects you, because you can't tell what's clean from what's dirty, and why should you have to inconvenience yourself by rummaging through her things to look? In such a case, you would tell her that you will no longer do her laundry unless she puts her dirty clothes in a hamper, either in a laundry room, a bathroom hamper, or some other designated place where you don't have to plow through her room and upset yourself.

The same thing holds for vacuuming her room. If you need to use a metal detector before you can safely use the vacuum cleaner (due to all the paper clips, thumbtacks, and earring backs in the carpet), you *are* being affected. Let her take over the responsibility for vacuuming her own room if she's not willing to delitter her floor.

Likewise, if a mess in her room is creating an odor that can be smelled when you walk by her door, or if ants and other insects are being drawn to her room because of spilled or leftover food, you and the rest of the household *are* being affected. In such a case, you would ground her until the room is thoroughly cleaned.

Fortunately, there is a compromise available between vigilantly monitoring your teen's room on a daily basis and just relaxing all standards and letting your teen take the consequences. You can set your mind at ease that a reasonable standard of cleanliness is maintained by requiring your teen to clean her room to an agreed-upon standard *once a week*. As with the behavior contract for other chores, if your teen doesn't clean her room by the weekly deadline you and she have agreed on, she loses all privileges until the room is cleaned. For example, if she doesn't meet the "Thursday at nine o'clock" deadline you've established and she wants to go to a pep rally the next afternoon right after school, she'll have to sit up late cleaning her room unless she wants to miss the pep rally.

However, this tactic doesn't solve the problem of the difference in perception you and your teen might have about what exactly constitutes a "clean room." To be sure that you are both on the same wavelength, and to save many arguments, specify the criteria for a clean room, write them down, and let your teen hang the list in her room. The list might include: making the bed with fresh linens, having all items of clothing hung or folded in closets or drawers, all furniture surfaces dusted with items neatly arranged, wastebasket clean and empty, carpet vacuumed, and nothing on the floor that shouldn't be there.

Obviously, you might not require all of these things, especially if you have household cleaning help. The point is that you and your teen must determine what needs to be on the list in order to set a clear expectation. (A similar list is also helpful for clarifying what a "clean kitchen" or a "clean bathroom" means.)

THE ALLOWANCE

You've been giving spending money to sixteen-year-old Sean whenever he needs it. Now he has a girlfriend and a car, and he's constantly hitting you up for extra money for dates and gas. You're wondering if you might not be better off giving him a set allowance that he can learn to budget.

Most teens who are on the "just ask for money when you need it" system don't want an allowance. They realize that they've got a good thing going, especially if their parents tend to be generous. This policy, however, doesn't teach them a thing about money management. And parents eventually realize that they are being ten-dollared to death!

Actually, it's wise to put a youngster on an allowance long before he's a teenager. He learns about spending, saving, making choices, and delayed gratification. But it's never too late to start an allowance system, and doing so when your son is a teenager will help prepare him for budgeting himself when he leaves home.

The amount of allowance, of course, depends on what you can afford and what a teen will be doing with it. For instance, if he's going to be paying for dates, gas for his car, and school lunch money, he'll need more money than the teen whose parents give him a gas allowance on their credit card and whose school lunches are charged to an account. Consequently, the amount of allowance can vary from a small weekly amount of "just for fun" money, all the way to a large monthly sum that includes money for all of your teen's expenses, including clothing.

If your teen has never had an allowance, or if he has and has been the type of kid who blows it all on his stomach, you're probably best to stick to a weekly allowance. As he matures and shows that he can be responsible with money, you can graduate him to a monthly sum, requiring him to budget more. You might want to encourage your older teen to start a checking account, giving him the opportunity to learn all about deposits, service charges, overdrafts, and checkbook balancing before he begins college or a full-time job.

The exact amount of allowance is something to be worked out in each individual case. Ask your teen what he thinks is a reasonable amount, what should be included as *his* expenses, and, perhaps, what he's willing to do for it. You may be a parent who feels strongly that your son should work for an allowance and not be given one just because he's breathing. In many families, allowing a teen to earn a larger allowance by his agreeing to do more household chores works out well.

In addition to giving your teen a set allowance, you might also allow him to earn extra money by doing special jobs around the house. Extra yard work, washing windows, cleaning rain gutters, washing the car, cleaning out a closet, putting the garage in order, and helping with household repairs provide opportunities for a teen to earn extra money when he needs it. Be clear, however, that you've agreed the job needs to be done; you probably don't want your car washed daily just so that he can get more spending money!

You'll probably also encounter times when your teen asks for an advance on all or part of his allowance. Give him the benefit of the doubt the first time he asks (if you have the money to give him), trusting that he will pay it back. At the time he borrows the money, be sure to specify exactly when he will repay the debt. If you find that you have trouble collecting, let your teen know that you'll no longer advance him money for a while; in a couple of months, you'll reconsider, based on his demonstration of responsibility with his money in the meantime.

Obviously, no matter how well calculated an allowance amount, there will be times when you'll want to give your teen a little extra. This becomes a problem only if a teen begins to expect that you will dole out extra funds anytime he asks, but should not interfere with your being flexible when circumstances warrant it.

MUSIC AND POSTERS

Fifteen-year-old Travis has started listening to music that you consider questionable and is covering his walls with weird-looking posters from these musical groups. You can barely understand the words these groups are singing, except for the obscenities that are liberally sprinkled throughout, and you're wondering if you should intervene in your teen's musical selections.

If your teen does not seem to be unduly affected by his musical choices, and basically remains his usual self, there's probably no reason to raise the issue and create a potential power struggle. On the other hand, if his new musical heroes seem to be part of a negative new identity, it would be wise to intervene.

Ask your teen to let you see and/or hear the CDs (with his translation if necessary). Many are packaged with a printout of the words to each song on the disc, so you might not have to listen to the music itself. And be aware that your teen can download music from the Internet as well. If you consider the music to contain objectionable content, you can take it away from him. You can also ban posters and T-shirts representing any of the offensive groups. Be sure to go to the trouble of checking out the lyrics themselves so that your teen cannot accuse you of judging a book (CD) by its cover. Also, not all loud music that teens love contains objectionable content.

After understanding the music's message and finding it objectionable, tell your teen *why* you consider it to be unsuitable. Since much of it conveys a rebellious, angry stance toward "the establishment" or the world, you'll want to explore whether or not your teen might be embracing such a philosophy. Is he rebellious, apathetic, or depressed? If so, why does this new identity he's trying to form hold such fascination for him? Again, it may take consultation with a mental health professional to determine exactly what's going on with your teen.

Realize, of course, that you can forbid the music, posters, T-shirts, and other paraphenalia associated with these music groups *in your house,* but you have no control over what your teen listens to when he is away from your supervision. It's likely that he'll continue to find ways to listen to what you've forbidden via his friends and the radio; it's a change in his negative identity that should be your primary concern.

PARENTAL SUPERVISION

Fifteen-year-old Brenda is working on you to allow her to give an unchaperoned party. She claims that "all the other parents do it" and that she'll be considered a nerd if her parents embarrass her by being present.

It's perfectly normal for teens not to want their parents "hanging around" when they have friends over, especially for a party. But don't give in to the pressure! Even if the parents of your teen's friends are allowing unchaperoned parties in their homes, you don't have to.

The fact is that too many problems can surface at an unchaperoned teen party, even if your teen has no intention of breaking your house rules. A friend may bring in alcohol and/or drugs, even though your daughter would not sanction it. Even if the invited friends all intend to abide by the rules you've set for your home, uninvited teens might try to crash the party. Word can get around quickly that a party is occuring and that no parents are in attendance.

Adolescents usually don't realize that they may need an adult present just to stay in control of an unplanned problem situation. Even with the best of intentions, can your daughter resist peer pressure and ask a friend to leave who's disobeying your house rules? And can she open the door to uninvited guests and keep them from entering the house? Let her know that it's much better to have an adult around to play the "heavy" in such circumstances.

Even if your teen is asking to have an unchaperoned party that's not coed, know that all the problems already mentioned can easily occur even at an all-girl party. Not only that, but boys have a way of showing up, with or without the girls' permission! If both sexes are present at a party, there's also a possibility that one or more of the "couples" will become sexually involved if an adult isn't around to monitor the situation.

You'll also want to explain to your teen about your liability should anything problematic occur during her party. For example, if a teen is served alcohol at your house and ends up being hurt or killed in a car accident after leaving your premises, you are liable for the damages. Even if a teen remains at your house, becomes drunk, and hurts another teen, you are also liable for the injury. Or if a teen gets alcohol poisoning from drinking in your home, you are held responsible for any resulting medical problems, including a victim's possible death. Likewise, if a teen is raped in your home, you can be held responsible for its occurence. Of course, your teen will accuse you of being totally paranoid for mentioning these unpleasant realities. But they still need to be stated.

Also, if you refuse to allow the unchaperoned party, be prepared for the fact that your teen will probably accuse you of not trusting her or her friends. Even though you calmly explain what can happen, don't expect her to agree with you. Remember, adolescents have that maddening sense that they are invulnerable, and that "it can't happen to me!" This situation represents a beautiful example of how being a good parent will not always grant you appreciation from your teen, or popularity with her friends.

Although you'll insist that an adult be present at the party, be sensitive to your adolescent's concern about your presence. Some parents try to enter into the party as if they are part of their teen's peer group, embarrassing her by being intrusive. So don't plan to stay in the area where the kids are gathered for any length of time, and don't join the group, unless you are specifically invited. In other words, stay out of view most of the time! But make it clear that you are there, and that you're awake and alert, by occasionally walking into the kitchen and/or by checking the food supply in the area where the party is taking place. The idea is that yo want to respect your teen's wish for privacy, yet make it apparent that you are around, if needed.

You might be wondering at what age you could allow your older teen to have a party at your house without your supervision. This decision is hard to call and very much depends on your teen's level of maturity as well as the trust you've developed with her. Even if she's moved out but comes home for vacation from college or for overnight visits, your house rules regarding alcohol, drugs, and so on need to be respected.

"CAN I HAVE THE CAR?"

Kevin will turn sixteen next week and plans to make a beeline to the Department of Motor Vehicles right after school on his birthday. He can't wait to get his driver's license, but you're not so eager to see this day arrive!

You'll probably feel ambivalent at best about your teen's getting a driver's license. On the one hand, it's a relief that he can now drive himself, and maybe his siblings, to school, lessons, meetings, sports events, and all those other activities for which you or your spouse have been the family chauffeur. He can also help you run errands on occasion.

The downside, of course, is that you're worried to death about how responsible a driver he'll be. The fact that his youth might give him quicker reflexes may be little consolation for the fact that teenagers tend to take risks, often combined with poor judgement. If he doesn't have access to a car of his own, you know you're in for some potential battles over when he can drive your car. But most of all, you sense, correctly, that your teen has reached another landmark that gives you even less control over his whereabouts and activities.

You may be in a better position to judge your son's driving abilities if he's had a learner's permit that has allowed him to operate a car in your presence over the pasr year. In fact, many parents allow their teens to take a driver's education course as soon as they are old enough to have a permit, specifically so that the teen will get many months of practice driving and so that the parent can observe the teen's driving ability firsthand as a passenger. Of course, it would be naive to assume that a teen will drive exactly the same way with a parent in the car as he might drive on his own, but giving your adolescent practice in driving before he goes solo can give you useful information about his driving skills.

It's wise to discuss the house rules concerning the car before your teen gets his license. If he's had driving experience via a learner's permit for many months before turning sixteen, and you feel comfortable with his driving ability, you might give him his independence with the car (assuming he has ready access to one). Of course, you might set some limitations, such as his not taking the car out of town without your permission.

If your teen has little driving experience, or if you are uncomfortable with his driving ability, you'll want to structure a system that allows him to use the car for specific purposes, increasing the frequency and distance he'll drive as he demonstrates that he will drive responsibly. For example, at first you might allow him only to drive to school, within a certain distance of the house, and/or only in daylight. You might require that he not have friends accompany him for a while, until he gets driving experience.

Of course, your adolescent is likely to balk at these initial restrictions. So you'll want to lay out a plan that makes it clear when his privileges will be increased, and under what circumstances.

You'll also want to let your teen know the consequences you will set (in addition to whatever legal measures are involved) for driving infractions or for the abuse of car privileges. These would include speeding tickets, moving violations, accidents, inappropriate parking (and towing), taking the car without permission (if you've set such limits), or driving to a place that you've designated as off-limits. Make it clear that you will hold him responsible for these infractions, including the financial obligations that can result.

For example, if your adolescent gets a speeding ticket, encourage him to take defensive driving, if that is an option available to him. If a fee is required, help him find a way to pay for it himself rather than writing out a check and handing it to him. You might also consider restricting his car privileges for a period of time, especially if he was driving at a highly inappropriate rate of speed. Likewise, if a car is damaged whike he is driving it, he will assume responsibility for getting it fixed (or for paying the deductible on the insurance policy). Whether you will also restrict his driving privileges for a period of time will depend on the degree of his responsiblity for the damage to the car. It might be that he won't drive again until he is able to pay off the debt for repairs.

Realize that you have one very definite advantage in your teen's being able to drive: *leverage!* Even if he has his own car, make it clear from the beginning that the privilege of driving it is still in your control, at least until he is no longer a minor.

FAMILY SECRETS

You're pleased that seventeen-year-old Meg has confided in you about her recent speeding ticket. But then she begs you not to tell her father, who tends to be the much stricter parent.

What a bind to be in! You're glad your daughter is being open with you, yet she's asking you to keep something important from your spouse. Even worse, you sympathize with her, because you suspect that your mate will react unreasonably (by your standards) when the secret is disclosed.

Difficult as it might be to tell your spouse about your teen's ticket (or any other thing she might want kept secret), you have much to lose if you follow her wishes. A parent who agrees to keep a secret (other than for surprise gifts or events) from the other parent forms an unhealthy collision with his teenager and, unintentionally or not, sets up a barrier with his spouse. The spouse's authority and feelings are undermined, and the teen has been allowed to put a wedge between her parents.

There are, however, some exceptions to this general rule. When the other parent is abusive, a parent is correct to put the teen's physical safety above rules for ideal family communication. Also, there are occasions when the other parent may be ill or terribly emotionally upset, making it wise to postpone the telling of an incident with a teen that could increase the stress on that parent.

But what if you perceive your spouse to be nonabusive but "impossible," perhaps highly unreasonable and/or overly uptight? If you think your spouse fits this description, it could be helpful for both of you to consult a mental health professional for counseling. It may be that some compromise between your points of view can be reached with the help of an objective party, and this would be highly preferable to keeping important information about your teen from your mate.

A parent who agrees to keep a teen's secret when she's under eighteen, or even if she's nineteen but still lives at home, usually feels caught in the middle between the teen and the spouse in many situations, and is likely to play the thankless role of the family peacemaker. The parent who is not privy to the secret commonly feels left out of the parenting role, alienated from the spouse, and resentful of the whole experience.

The best way not to get yourself into such a situation is to make it clear from your teen's childhood on that you won't keep secrets from your spouse. It might not seem like a big deal to keep your third-grader's poor test grade a secret, but it is just this kind of "small thing" that sets up the expectation that you'll continue keeping bigger secrets when your child becomes an adolescent.

But suppose you have kept secrets in the past. It's never too late to let your teenager know that you'll no longer do this. Encourage her to tell the other parent what has happened, perhaps helping her to formulate how she will do this and what she will say. Suggest that she might tell your mate, "I need to talk to you about something, but it's hard for me to do it because I'm afraid you'll get very angry. But I know you'd rather I tell you the truth, even if it's upsetting, wouldn't you?" This kind of statement usually results in the listener's making an effort to stay in emotional control.

Let your teenager know that it's usually much better to confront someone with bad news about oneself rather than having someone else do it for her. But be clear that if she refuses to tell her other parent, you will do it for her. Remember that kids of all ages do better with parents who communicate openly, make joint parenting decisions whenever possible, and demonstrate respect for each other's position even when they disagree.

THE INTERNET

Thirteen-year-old Caroline spends a lot of time on her computer, and you notice that she's becoming unusually eager to rush to it as soon as she gets home. Plus she's also started hitting the delete key whenever you walk into her room. Emptying out her wastebasket one day, you discover a printout of her e-mail correspondence with a man you've never heard of. It's clear that the two of them are planning to set up a meeting.

The Internet has become both a blessing and a curse to parents. On the one hand, it opens up extraordinary opportunities for learning and research. On the other, it can expose children and teens to all sorts of people and information that can be considered inappropriate if not downright dangerous.

Teens, of course, are both trusting and naive. They can give out all sorts of information about themselves and their families without realizing the potential for trouble if the information gets into the wrong hands. Whether from their rebellion or their idealism, they can be drawn to causes and groups that run totally counter to their parents' beliefs and values. On the Web, they can click on sites about pornography, violence, and bigotry, or to pedophiles and the "fringe elements" of our society.

Two concerns surface. First, the time issue. Many youngsters are so caught up in the "virtual world" of the Internet that they sacrifice opportunities for "real life" experiences. The computer begins to interfere with grades, family time, and healthy activities. Online chat rooms replace live interaction. Consequently, parents need to set limits on the amount of time spent on the computer–with exceptions for genuine information-gathering that is necessary for schoolwork.

The second concern is supervision. Many teens are home–at least for a few hours a day–without a parent being present. Even if a parent is home when a teen is using the computer, how can an adult monitor her Internet activity without becoming an obsessive snoop?

Truth is, many parents aren't nearly as informed about computers as their teens. Parents can think they've made it impossible for their teens to access unacceptable Internet sites, while their more technologically-savvy teens simply program their way around their parents' efforts!

Fortunately, parents have access to a variety of software that will block access to objectionable material. Of course, what is "objectionable" to one parent might not be to another, so some research is necessary to decide which software best fits with parental values. Many of these software programs also provide a method for parents to check and see what their teens are accessing. To find out about these software options, type "Internet parental control" into a search engine and check out the various offerings.

The bottom line is that computer usage is a privilege that can be both granted and taken away (just like the telephone, the car, and the CD player). When a teen violates the working agreement about computer use, she should be barred from using her PC for a specified time period.

It is wise to discuss rules of Internet usage with your teen before it becomes a problem. One rule might be that she can't communicate with anyone on the Internet without your permission. Even in an "approved" chat room, she can't give out your telephone number or address unless she's checked with you first.

If you find that your teen is communicating with anyone you do not approve of, forbid the contact. Let the "other party" communicate with you if he or she wants permission to continue Internet chats with your teen. A "legitimate" person would be happy to speak to a teen's parents.

SIX

SCHOOL AND WORK

Parents typically want their young children to do well in school. But as their offspring become adolescents and move into high school they are likely to become even more concerned with a teen's academic achievement. If there is an expectation that college lies ahead, the pressure increases even more, both for the teen and for the parents.

Obviously, parents would love for their teens to qualify for scholarships, making higher education more affordable. They can become especially frustrated if the adolescent has high academic potential yet gets less-than-spectacular grades. Even if scholarships are not in sight, or a quest for a prestigious college is not an issue, parents still want their teens to make high enough grades to qualify for college entrance *somewhere*. Of course, just because parents *want* a teen to go to college doesn't guarantee that the teen will want to go.

Even if parents aren't concerned about a teen's going to college, they want her to make good enough grades in high school to ensure that she'll graduate. They realize that teens who consistently get low or failing marks are at high risk of becoming dropouts.

Most parents are not so concerned about their teen's picking a specific career, but want their adolescent to begin thinking about interests and abilities that will become a focus for a later career choice. Some parents, in their concern for their teenager's future, will begin to put premature pressure on their older adolescent to figure out what she "wants to do with her life." A few teens will know exactly what job or career they want. Many will have a rough idea of what they *think* they want to do. And some will have no earthly idea!

Conflicts can also occur about a teen's potential choice of job or career, if one has been selected. Parents may unintentionally project their own frustrated desires on their teen and then be disappointed when she selects a field that's totally different from what they had hoped. They may expect that she will go into a family business or profession, yet she may have no desire to do so. Or a teen might decide to follow a goal that a parent considers to be an impractical or unrealistic dream.

If you have one of these conflicts with your adolescent, you'll need to remain realistic and positive. If you become critical of her wishes, you'll only interrupt the flow of communication between you and have even less impact on her decisions.

COMMON DILEMMAS

CHANGING A REPORT CARD

You're shocked when you find out that fourteen-year-old Betsy changed her math grade on her report card from a D to a B. You are utterly dismayed that she tried to deceive you.

Rather than launching into an angry tirade or an emotional display of your disappointment in her behavior, your best approach is to remain as calm as you can and try to find out what motivated your teen's deception. Did her changing the grade stem from her own shame about making such a low mark or from her fear of how you, or her other parent, might react?

If she's used to making high grades, she might be embarrassed about making a D. Admitting her poor performance to herself could be bad enough, but to have anyone else know about it might seem too humiliating. If this is the case, you'll want to help your daughter examine her expectations about herself. After all, her worth as a person is not dependent on her grades.

If her falsifying the grade was motivated by fear of your reaction, is she afraid of a specific punishment (having to be grounded the weekend of the Homecoming dance), being punished unreasonably (a severe restriction), and/or is she worried about disappointing you ("I thought you'd be upset because I might not get a scholarship")? A good way to find this out is to ask, "What do you think would have happened if you'd shown me a report card with a D on it?"

If you *automatically* take away a teen's weekend privileges when she makes a low grade, you increase the possibility that she'll be untruthful if an important event is coming up the weekend after the grade is disclosed. Although immature, her reaction is likely to be focused on the short-term consequence. This is the reason many teens will conceal a bad progress note or a poor report card until "next week"; they know they risk their parents' being more angry for the deception, but they'd rather take their bitter medicine *later* than miss something important that's coming up in their *immediate* future.

Because of this common teen reaction, it's usually best to gear your negative consequence for a low grade, if there is to be one, to non–school evenings (e.g., a set study period every night during which the teen will not use the phone, or removing the teen's television from her room until the grade improves). If you decide you must limit her weekend activities, be flexible and allow her some choice (e.g., she can only go out one weekend night, but can choose which one; she can choose to be grounded the following weekend if this one is special).

You might also ask yourself whether you are a difficult parent when it comes to handling "bad news." For example, do you explode, not speak to your teen for hours (or days), give excruciating lectures, or berate your teen when she tells you something you don't like to hear? If so, you increase the likelihood that an adolescent might try to deceive you. Of course, this doesn't sanction her deception, but it does make it more understandable.

If you find that your teen felt she couldn't tell you the truth because you would be so disappointed in her, you'll need to examine your own expectations. It's one thing to let her know that you are disappointed in her decisions or actions, but another to make her feel that *she* is a terrible disappointment to you. Admittedly, this can be a hard line to draw at times, so you'll want to give your adolescent lots of evidence that you love her, even when she makes mistakes.

You can accomplish this by remaining compassionate toward her when she does make one, by giving her the message with your *attitude* that you expect her to learn from mistakes, and by admitting that you've also made them. It can be helpful to make statements like "Honey, all people make mistakes, the important thing is to learn something from this experience," or "When I've done something I wish I hadn't, I try to figure out what the lesson is in the experience and learn from it." If you maintain this stance, your teen won't be so likely to question her own worth as a person, or your love for her, when she's used poor judgment or done something that she shouldn't.

Even though your teen changed her grade, the severity of the consequence you give her, if there is one, needs to depend on whether this is a first offense, the reason for the low mark, and what her attitude is about her deception. If her low mark resulted from ignoring homework or refusing to study, you'll feel differently than if she had put forth maximum effort but had genuine difficulty. If she clearly feels bad about what she did (rather than feeling bad about being caught), she might not need a consequence, especially for a first offense.

Obviously, your teen's behavior has been a breach of trust. You'll want to let her know, as with any other time trust has been violated, that she will have to earn your trust back over a period of time, no matter what the reason for her changing the grade.

(Much of this same discussion would also apply to the teen who cheats on a test.)

SKIPPING SCHOOL

*The attendance office calls to tell you that sixteen-year-old Barry
has not been in school for the past two days.*

You're likely to feel baffled, angry, and/or frightened when you
discover that your teen isn't going to school. Your first panicky
thoughts are likely to be "What's happened? Where *is* he, and what
is he doing when he's not in school?"

Obviously, adolescents might not go to school for many reasons. They might be avoiding something, or someone, at school.
They might be skipping out for mischievous fun with a friend, or
to help a friend with a problem. Or they might be involved in more
serious activity, such as alcohol or drug use. They might also be
feeling too confused, overwhelmed, or depressed to handle school
and are trying to sort out their feelings.

Remember that even though you are likely to be very upset
when you find out your teen is not going to school, your goal is to
find out what is going on with him and to get him back in school.
It's only natural to feel angry and to convey this with your body
language and, perhaps, a stern voice tone. Yet it won't help to lose
your temper and shut down communication. If you still feel angry
after you've found out the details of your adolescent's behavior, you
can let him know that in the context of rational discussion. But
before you know the facts, you'll want to stay as calm as you can
so that your teen will open up and talk honestly with you.

When your teen comes home, supposedly from school, be up
front with him about the fact that you know he hasn't been there.
If you've tracked him down before he's come home, don't try to
talk to him in front of his friends or in public, but wait until the
two of you are alone or, perhaps, with the other parent.

Find a private place that's comfortable before you talk things
over. If your teen is angry and noncommunicative, you might tell
him he can go to his room to be alone for a while or to calm down
and that the two of you will talk in thirty minutes or at some other
specified time. There's no point in trying to force him to talk just

at that moment, so let him collect his thoughts to maximize the chance that he'll be more receptive a little later. You may also need such a break in order to contain your own anger.

Tell your teen that you'd like to hear from him first about his skipping school, as you don't want to jump to any hasty conclusions. Rather than giving him your opinions, advice, feelings, interpretations, and conclusions, just encourage him to talk to you. You'll ask him, if he doesn't volunteer the information, what led up to his decision to skip school, and to account for his whereabouts while he was absent.

If your adolescent is having a problem with school itself, suggest that the two of you set up a conference with the counselor or principal, or perhaps an involved teacher, to resolve the issue. If he confides that he's having emotional problems, and talking things out with you doesn't provide direction or relief, consult with a mental health professional.

If he's been skipping school with one or more friends, your decision about the consequences will depend, of course, on their activities. It's wise to check out your teen's story with appropriate sources (the other teen's parents, the school, a police report, the place where your teen says he was staying) before you make a final determination about what occurred. If it seems your teen was involved in innocent mischief or adventure "as a kick," and it's a first offense, you might just set up an appropriate restriction (loss of some privilege, or a grounding, for a specified time period). If he's been engaged in illegal or dangerous activities, such as experimenting with drugs or alcohol, you would set a more severe restriction, perhaps including the stipulation that he cannot socialize after school or on weekends with that particular friend or group of friends for some time after the general restriction has been lifted.

If this is your son's first offense of this type, if you believe that his drinking and/or drug use was mild and experimental, and if you feel that he is well adjusted in general, you wouldn't necessarily need to see a mental health professional at this point. You would let him know very clearly what your policy will be if he *continues* to use alcohol or drugs.

Obviously, if you have reason to believe that your son is into heavy alcohol or drug use, even if this is the first time you've found out about such activity, consultation with a mental health professional is strongly recommended. (For more information about alcohol and drug issues, see Chapter Eight.)

No matter what the reason for your teen's skipping school, let him know that he must go back immediately. If he tells you he's emotionally upset about something, you might be tempted to let him stay home a few days, thinking a rest from school could help him feel better. This decision is almost always a mistake. The longer a teen is out of school, the more difficult it is to get him to go back. If he refuses to go back, immediately schedule an appointment with a mental health professional. Let the receptionist know that you have an adolescent who is refusing to go to school, as this situation is usually considered an emergency and should get you in to see the professional very quickly.

THE HOMEWORK HASSLE

For fourteen-year-old Jill, her social life is much more important than her schoolwork. When you ask her why she rarely studies at home, she insists that she does her homework at school. Now you've just received a progress note stating that she's in danger of failing several subjects because—you guessed it—she's not completing her assignments!

First, you want to determine what is getting in the way of your teen's doing homework. Is she spending too much time on the phone, or watching television? Is she involved in too many extracurricular activities? If either of these seems to be the problem, you might simply limit such activities for a few weeks and see if her grades improve.

Of course, many parents are faced with the problem of not being able to monitor their teen's after-school (or, sometimes, evening) activities because their work schedules prevent their being home. If a parent can't spend a reasonable amount of time at home in the afternoon or evening, it may be necessary to create an alternative solution. Some parents have required teens to spend after-school time at a relative's, or even at their own workplace, if possible. Sometimes, a younger teen can be supervised by a college student who is paid to spend an hour to two monitoring and assisting with the teen's homework. Or a teen can be required to spend time at a public library; the library atmosphere is often conducive to getting a teen to settle in and complete homework.

Another effective approach, especially if the problem continues, is to make a teen's weekend privileges depend on her completing homework. A simple way to do this is to establish a "Friday report system": She takes a paper to school with the heading "I Have No Missing Assignments," followed by a list of her classes and a column for teacher signatures; she presents the paper at the end of each class and asks the teacher to initial the appropriate column.

When she brings the report home each Friday, she gets all of her normal weekend privileges if there are no missing assignments in any class. If one is missing, you might allow her to have her privileges *only* after she completes the missing assignment and shows it to you. If more than one assignment is missing, her weekend privileges are forfeited. If you don't want to use weekend privileges as the incentive, you could substitute the privilege of her having her phone, television, or stereo in her room for the *next* week. If you had to remove one of these for a negative Friday report, she would be able to earn it back with a positive report the next Friday. Of course, you could also use a combination of these two incentives/consequences.

No doubt there will be a time when your teen will arrive home on Friday without a report from one or more teachers, perhaps with an excuse (legitimate or otherwise) that she had a substitute teacher who wouldn't sign the report, that circumstances prevented her from getting to the teacher that day, or that she misplaced the report. Ask her to tell you what the report *would* have said, give her the benefit of the doubt, and ask her to bring the report on Monday. Let her know, however, that if you don't get the report Monday, you'll call the teacher(s) to check things out for yourself. If you find out that your teen has not told the truth, you'll not be able to trust her word about the Friday report. From then on, a missing or incomplete Friday report results in her forfeiting the agreed-on privileges *until* she brings the report home.

Most teens are not thrilled about this system, so let your adolescent know that you will drop it after several weeks of her proving to you that she's completing her assignments. Be sure she understands that it is her responsibility, not the teacher's or the counselor's, to make up the report and to get it signed. Most teachers are happy to cooperate with this system since it takes only a moment of their time to initial the paper, but you certainly should check with the school counselor or teacher before implementing such a plan. In some instances, the counselor may have her own system for collecting such information and can relay the results to you.

A nice feature of the "Friday report" is that it gives you a way to know whether or not your teenager is completing her assignments without having to nag her throughout the week about homework. Also, if the system is followed, she'll salvage her grades by not getting too far behind.

You might wonder why it is suggested that you target "completing assignments" rather than grades on the report. The reason is that most teens who fail courses do so because of missing assignments. A zero averaged with a 100 winds up being a 50, so even a few instances of not turning in homework can play havoc with a grade point average. Also, it is very time-consuming for a teacher to have to average a student's grades every week. So if you do target grades for the Friday report, consider asking the teachers to note that the teen is "passing" a subject.

Sometimes a student will have a homework problem only in one class. She might not like the teacher or the subject, or she might find the work to be difficult or boring. If this is the case, you could implement the "Friday report" only for that one class.

If your teen really balks at using a reporting system, ask her to come up with an alternative plan for bringing up her grades. If she vows to reform, or thinks of a sensible alternative plan, you might give her a chance to show that she will follow through with her suggestion. If not, insist that she begin the reporting system.

GREAT POTENTIAL, POOR ACHIEVEMENT

Sixteen-year-old Mark has a superior IQ, but remains totally un-interested in his schoolwork. His grades remain mediocre, and nothing you've tried has resulted in motivating him to do better in school.

First, you'll want to make sure that your son's lack of motivation doesn't stem from a physical problem, so you'll want to have him evaluated by a physician. Then you'll want to check his scores on achievement tests given in school the past few years. Even though he's bright, he might still have an undiagnosed learning difference; low achievement scores would raise this possibility and indicate that a thorough educational evaluation is in order. You'll also want to consider whether or not your teen's lack of motivation reflects "acting out" toward you or an underlying depression. If you think this is possible, consultation with a mental health professional is recommended.

Next, you'll want to implement a privilege/consequence system to see if you can raise your teen's motivation to do schoolwork. Set up a behavior contract with him whereby improved grades result in some privilege that is important to him.

But what happens if you've done all these things and nothing has worked? Your teen still sloughs off schoolwork, and the two of you are locked into an angry standoff about it. At this point, it might be best to take a totally different approach: Let your adolescent assume total responsibility for his school achievement (or lack of it). Tell him that you would like him to get better grades in school, but that it's not worth ruining your relationship with him by bugging him continually about schoolwork. Consequently, you'll no longer even ask about his grades, homework, or tests. If he would like your help with one of his class subjects, or if he wants to discuss a problem related to classwork, you'll be glad to do what you can to help him out.

Tell him that you know he's very bright and capable and that the time will arrive when he'll become interested in some course of study or career field. You know that he'll do fine when this time comes and that he'll have no trouble motivating himself to do whatever's required for him to be successful.

Then comes the hard part: living up to your end of the bargain! Many parents *say* they're going to leave all schoolwork issues up to their teen, bite their tongues a few times, but then can't resist mentioning the upcoming report card or the fact that he hasn't cracked a book in a week. This behavior, of course, destroys the intent of the whole approach.

If you decide to use this tactic, it's very important that you do so without any aura of resentment toward or disappointment with your adolescent. You want to give him the positive message that you have faith in him and in his abilities and that you are not holding a grudge about his choosing to underachieve in school. He's well aware that you would strongly prefer him to actualize his academic potential, but he needs to feel that you still consider him to be a great kid even if he doesn't.

Sometimes just removing the pressure about schoolwork and grades will result in your teen's putting more effort into his studies. If he's been resentful of your longtime expectation that he should make high grades due to his tremendous potential, he'll no longer have reason to rebel.

More than likely, however, your teen's academic efforts will remain unchanged, at least for a while. His interest in academics may bloom later on in high school, or once he begins college. He might start college, drop out, work a while, and then go back. Many very successful adults have become excellent students when they *return* to college, as they return to school highly motivated. And, of course, he may become successful without ever going to college.

It's true that if you take this approach with your teen, you'll probably never see him graduate as valedictorian of his high school, nor watch him be inducted into the National Honor Society. Nor is he likely to receive a plethora of academic scholarships. But giving him a clear message that his worth as a person is not dependent on his academic achievement will save you from alienating him, and preserve a mutually respectful relationship between you and your son.

OVERANXIOUS ABOUT GRADES

Sixteen-year-old Angela is driving herself crazy trying to maintain an A average. She worries continually about her grades and gets especially uptight before tests. You see her getting more and more stressed, but what can you do to help her?

Chances are that a teen who's overanxious about getting high grades is the type of person who wants to do her best in *everything*, otherwise known as a perfectionist. While it's admirable for a person to want to achieve, it should not be at the cost of worrying endlessly about one's performance. Perfectionists can literally make themselves sick with anxiety, and many suffer occasionally or chronically from stress-related physical problems.

You'll want to talk with your teen about the reasons why she is so concerned about making all A's. Perhaps she thinks that you will not regard her highly if her grades drop, or that you'll be disappointed in her. If she's always had "great potential," it's possible that you've unintentionally stressed her abilities so strongly that she thinks you'll be upset with her if she doesn't maintain a certain standard.

Even if you haven't pressured your teen directly about her grades, it may be that yours is a high-achieving family; the pressure is just there. You, your spouse, and/or a sibling might be high achievers, and your teen fears that she simply won't measure up. It's also possible that your teen is modeling your *own* striving for perfection. If you think this is the case, begin to poke a little fun at yourself when you get uptight about everything being done "just right." Let your teen know about a few mistakes you've made, or things you've done that haven't turned out spectacularly, and invite her to "catch" you when she sees you overworrying about something that is not of earth-shattering proportions.

You'll want to give your teen the message that you want her to do well, but not at the expense of her emotional or physical health. Remind her that many highly successful people in all types of professions and careers did not make exceptional grades in school. It can also help to point out that striving for perfection is an impossible goal: no matter how pretty, smart, or skilled one is, there will always be someone prettier, smarter, or more skilled. While it may seem obvious to you, be sure to tell her that you will not love her any less if she doesn't make outstanding grades.

Although it's unlikely that such conversation will remove completely the internal pressure your teen is experiencing, just giving her your direct permission to ease up on herself can encourage her to realign her priorities. When you see her becoming stressed, ask her to imagine "the worst thing" that could possibly happen if she doesn't do whatever it is that she thinks needs to be done so perfectly. Keep asking her "And then what would happen?" pointing out the natural consequence—and solution—for each thing she brings up. Usually, such an exercise ends up being humorous, as it's unlikely that "the worst thing" would even happen in the first place—and even if it did, it would not be a catastrophic event!

It's also very helpful to teach an overanxious teen some simple relaxation skills. There are many good books and tapes on the subject, but one of the simplest procedures to learn is the "progressive muscle relaxation" technique. It involves settling into a comfortable position in a quiet place, taking some deep breaths, and then breathing normally while tensing and then releasing the muscle groups of the body (from feet to head, or the reverse). With a little practice, your teen can learn to spend fifteen minutes or so using such a technique to calm herself whenever she feels the need for a relaxation break.

SCARED TO LOOK SMART

Fourteen-year-old Marty is a very bright teen who easily does well in school. But suddenly, in his freshman year in high school, he begins to make mediocre grades. When you confront him about the situation, he confides that he's embarrassed to look "too smart" to his peers.

Some teens get the idea that it is "nerdy" to excel academically. This is especially common with boys, but may also occur in girls.

Now that peers are becoming more important, teens will frequently go out of their way not to do something that they think will alienate them from their classmates.

It can be helpful to point out to your teen that excelling academically doesn't make a person a nerd. "Nerdy" behavior has more to do with social skills, and nerds can make all A's or all F's.

In the case where peers do make fun of an exceptional student, it is often because that student comes off as a know-it-all, or treats classmates as if they are inferior. The peer rejection is due to obnoxious or inconsiderate behavior, not to what appears on a report card.

TO WORK, OR NOT?

Now that Jordan has had her sixteenth birthday, she informs you that she wants to get a job after school to earn extra spending money. You're not so sure this is a good idea, as you wonder how a job might affect her academic performance and social life.

There are several factors to consider when deciding whether or not to allow your teen to get a job during the school years. First, you'll want to consider the effect a job might have on her grades. If she easily makes good grades, you might not worry that her working will significantly affect her report card. If she's the kind of student who has to work hard for her grades, you might feel that a job will intrude into her study time, and that her grades will fall. If she's a weak student, you obviously might worry about her ability to handle a job and still pass her courses.

Of course, there are some teens who perform at a mediocre level in school because they are totally unmotivated for academics. Having a job just might help to *improve* their grades because their parents could insist that they would have to maintain a certain minimum grade point average, or have no failing grades, if they wanted to continue the privilege of *keeping* their job. A teen who is strongly motivated to earn money might increase her efforts at school in order to be able to continue working. Also, if a teen isn't experiencing much success in school, having a job and earning money of her own might boost her self-esteem.

If your teen is involved in sports or other extracurricular activities, it's unlikely that she could add the demands of a job to her other commitments and still keep up her grades. But for the adolescent who is not involved in any constructive activity other than going to school, a job can provide a productive way to take up some of her free time. It can also give her a way to meet new friends if she's involved with a less-than-desirable group or if she lacks friends.

If you decide to allow your adolescent to get a job, make it clear that you consider her first priority to be her schoolwork. If she's a good student, you expect her to continue to be one. If her grades are just so-so, you don't want them to drop to F's. Consider limiting the number of hours she will spend at work, especially in the beginning, to see how things go. You might agree that the two of you will reevaluate the situation at the end of the next grading period to see if her work time needs to be cut back or, perhaps, can be increased.

You might also want to set limits on the kind of job your teen will have, the area of town in which she will work, and whether or not working after dark will be advisable based on the circumstances. These parameters may need to be negotiated just as were the house rules you've already established.

Don't be surprised if your teenager spends all of her earnings on items that you feel are frivolous or unnecessary. You might suggest that she put a certain amount of money aside for savings, perhaps for her education, or for a car. But it's best not to dictate the budgeting of her earnings. This is a great way for her to learn about spending, saving, and budgeting, and part of the lesson often involves making a few mistakes along the way.

DROPPING OUT

Seventeen-year-old Bart knocks on your door late one evening and says he needs to talk to you. He looks upset when he enters your bedroom, and finally blurts out, "I just wanted to let you know that I've decided to quit high school and get my GED!"

Typically, a parent feels shocked and dismayed by such an announcement. If your teen has been making mediocre or poor grades throughout high school, you might have worried that just this situation could happen one day. Or you might have been concerned that he might not go to college, but never dreamed that he wouldn't graduate from high school. Either way, you probably feel unprepared for the reality that this is actually happening.

While you might feel panicky, disappointed, frustrated, and/or angry, don't lecture, lash out, or threaten your teen. With as much calmness as you can muster, ask him why he is considering dropping out of school. Hear him out before you begin to give him your ideas on the matter.

Often, an older teen might make this decision after failing a course (or thinking he will fail it) and realizing that he can't graduate on time with the rest of his class. If this is the case, find out first if his conclusions are accurate. The school counselor may be able to offer some options: Your teen might be able to take a night class or a correspondence course that would allow him to graduate on time. If not, many schools allow seniors to participate in the graduation ceremony even though they get a "blank" diploma on stage, and then mail the real diploma after the student completes the graduation requirements in summer school. If these options apply, your son might be persuaded to change his mind.

Perhaps he's decided to quit school because he feels overwhelmed by his schoolwork. Academics may be genuinely hard for him, especially if achievement tests show that he's significantly below grade level. If he has no motivation to go to college, he may not see the point of staying in school. For this type of youngster, letting him enroll in a work-study or vocational program in his high school might allow him to experience some success while keeping him in school.

There's also a possibility that something unrelated to academics is happening at school that makes a teen want to drop out. It could be a negative reaction to a particular teacher, a social situation that's bothering him, or some personal issue that makes him uncomfortable. You'll want to draw him out to see if any of these are possibilities. Helpful questions include "What do you think is really bothering you about school?" "When did you begin feeling like you want to leave school?" "What are you worried might be hard for you if you stay in school?" and "Help me understand why it's important for you to drop out right now." Once he does tell you what the problem is, help him find a solution for his specific situation. This might even include allowing him to transfer to a different high school, if that's an option.

If your teen is determined to drop out, for whatever reason, you may have a difficult time convincing him that a high school diploma is better than a GED. He's probably already checked, and knows that he can still get into a junior college with a GED, if college is a goal for him. He may also know that he can still get into the military service with a GED, although you will want to point out that he may not be able to pick his field of interest, but must accept any assignment. Obviously, he can get a job with a GED, but he needs to know that most employers will still select a young person with a regular high school diploma over one with a GED, if they have a choice.

The fact is that the advantage of receiving a high school diploma over a GED is largely a subjective matter, albeit one that brings out a great deal of emotion in many parents. There is an intangible feeling in parents' minds that a GED represents "second best" for a teenager, that he somehow couldn't manage a regular high school curriculum. Even most teenagers will admit that they'd prefer getting a diploma rather than a GED, all other things being equal. But if a teen has his mind set on dropping out, a GED looks good enough.

If your teen cannot be convinced to remain in high school, and you're equally convinced that he should remain there, you might consider making some type of trade-off that would change his mind. Many parents feel that it's important enough for an adolescent to graduate to offer him a major incentive for doing so, such as a car, money for an after-graduation trip, and so on. This is a very personal decision, but many parents feel that the end justifies the means in such a case.

If you think that your teen will respond to an emotional plea that you can't stand the thought of not seeing him walk across the stage at graduation and that it would fill you with tremendous parental pride to watch him do so, you'll probably be disappointed with his response. A teen who's not motivated to graduate could usually care less about walking across the stage, or at least that's what he'll tell himself. He's likely to accuse the parent of being silly and/or of using guilt-inducing tactics just to manipulate him into doing something against his will.

If all efforts fail to convince your teen to remain in school, re-alize that this is not the end of the world (although it might well feel like it at the moment). Many older teens get GEDs and end up later on with good jobs, or they attend junior college and then go on to get four-year and/or advanced degrees. It may not be the traditional way to get an education, but it certainly doesn't mean that a young person will not be successful.

THE COLLEGE OPTION

It's a few months before Carrie's graduation from high school, and you are pleased that she's been accepted to three good colleges. When you ask her if she's made up her mind which school she will attend, she drops the bomb that she no longer wants to go to college!

It will be important to put your own feelings aside for the mo-ment so that you can help your teen sort out the reasons behind her statement. Is she just having a little normal insecurity about leaving home, growing up, and/or having to separate from a boy-friend? Or is it possible that she really might *not* be ready for col-lege?

A teen who is still quite dependent may have second thoughts about leaving home. She might worry that she'll be homesick for her family. Or she might worry about how she will fit in with a new group of people, especially if she is not going to be rooming with someone she knows. She might feel unsure about her academic abilities and wonder if she'll be able to handle the demands of a college curriculum. The best way to draw her out, if she doesn't volunteer the information, is to ask her directly about these issues. She'll be less likely to deny such problems if your attitude is supportive and nonjudgmental.

If your teen continues to have any of these concerns despite your efforts to reassure her, you might want to suggest that she attend a local college, at least for a year. That way she can test her wings with college academics without losing the security of her family, while also giving herself a little more time to mature before she leaves home. There's still plenty of time for her to go away to her preferred college.

If she's in love, and her boyfriend will be staying in town, she might understandably be uneasy about leaving him. This could occur because their relationship is going so well that she can't stand the thought of their being apart, or because things are *not* going well and she's afraid that a separation will lead to a breakup. Either way, it may be difficult to convince her to leave for college as long as this relationship exists.

Of course, her wish not to go to college could legitimately mean that she simply does not want to go. She may be tired and frustrated with school, or want to take a break before continuing her education. She may feel that her interests and goals aren't developed enough for her to select a specific course of study and may feel uneasy about going to school with no real sense of what she wants to do after graduation. And, of course, she may question whether or not college is really necessary for her.

If your teen continues to express a preference not to go to college, it's probably best not to insist that she go. Parents often worry that if a teen doesn't continue her formal education right after high school, she'll never go back to school. So they push her to enroll in college in spite of her wishes. However, if she attends college without genuine commitment, she's likely to waste both time and money.

Working for a year, probably at a minimum-wage job, often provides the best motivation for an older teen to decide to go back to school. When college is truly a matter of *her* choice—which may be a year after graduation from high school or several years later—she's likely to be a much more focused and conscientious student. Your money and/or hers will be put to far better use.

A DISAPPOINTING CAREER CHOICE

Nineteen-year-old Emily grew up anticipating the day she would be able to enter the family law practice. Now she's home for summer vacation from her freshman year at a prestigious college. You're shocked when she announces that she recently changed her major from prelaw to dance.

Some of the most difficult moments for parents occur when their fantasies about their teen get shattered. Whether it's an expectation that she will get more education or a higher-status job than the parent did, or that she will pursue a particular career, a parent's disappointment can run deep when the teen doesn't fulfill the parent's dream. When there is a family business, when a number of family members have traditionally followed a particular career path, the expectation is even more powerful.

A parent can get even more upset if an older teen's choice of career doesn't seem practical or doesn't provide the same level of professionalism, income, or status that the parent thinks is appropriate. If the adolescent has a particular talent or ability and then refuses to pursue it, the parent can feel even more frustrated and pained.

Whatever the source of the disappointment, a parent must acknowledge that such a feeling is the *parent's* problem, rather than the teen's. Even if it could be known in advance that a career choice is a mistake, it still remains the teen's choice to make it.

Although you might have to bite your tongue, you will gain better rapport with your teen by remaining positive rather than critical about her career choice. Of course, you'll point out its advantages and disadvantages, from your perspective. But you need to let her know that you do respect her wishes and preferences and that you will support whatever choice she makes.

By maintaining good rapport, you will leave the door open for ongoing discussion. If your teen realizes she's made a mistake, she'll then be more inclined to admit it and to let you help. If you are the one who turns out to be wrong, you'll both be able to enjoy her success and happiness without resentment on either side.

WHEN THE NEST IS TOO COZY

Nineteen-year-old Ron graduated from high school over a year ago. Since then he has occupied his time by sleeping late and hanging out with his friends until the wee morning hours. He enrolled in a couple of courses at the local junior college, but dropped one and got an incomplete in the other. He says that he can't find a job, and he refuses to check out the classified ads for jobs at fast-food places and supermarkets.

Sometimes a teen simply refuses to grow up. He continues to let his parents support him, won't work or go to school, and does little or nothing to help out around the house. When confronted about his lack of responsibility, he offers excuses and blames his circumstances on everyone but himself.

Many times the solution to this problem is obvious to everyone but the parent(s) of the teen: cutting off his funds! After all, he has to have money in order to get haircuts, put gas in the car, and go out with his friends. Yet his parents continue to provide these things for him, perhaps even buying his clothes, paying for his membership to a health club, and maybe even sending him on a nice vacation. They may lecture, yell, and threaten him, but the bottom line is that they continue paying for him to lead his usual lifestyle.

If you should find yourself in this position with your older teen, arrange a time when the two of you can talk. You might want to hold this discussion away from the house, where there will be no distractions and where you will have a captive audience (in a restaurant, on a long drive, etc.). Let him know that you realize you've been doing him a disservice by allowing him to remain dependent on you long past the appropriate age for him to begin his adult journey.

Tell him that you want to draw up a contract with him that specifies the conditions under which you will allow him to remain at home and for how long a time period. For example, you might agree to continue supporting him *if* he enrolls in a full college or vocational course load, or if he takes one or two classes *and* works so many hours a week. Let him know that you will not pay for the same course twice; if he fails one or gets an incomplete, *he* will pay the tuition to repeat that course. If he is not interested in continuing his education, then he must get a full-time job. Set a deadline that will allow him a reasonable period of time in which to find work, and let him know that all funds from you will stop on that day.

Then comes the hard part: following through. No doubt you've already told him some of these same things before, but kept extending the deadline. He needs to see that you mean business and that the free ride is over.

When the money runs out (with no "extras" even for a birthday or other holiday when you've usually given him money), most teens will find a way to earn some money and/or move out. They might move in with a friend and still not work or go to school for a while. Eventually, of course, they will run out of friends who will continue to support them. Once they are out of your house, however, there is likely to be much less tension and hassle in your relationship.

Some teens, of course, will remain openly angry about your having "kicked them out," perhaps severing communication with you (or threatening to do so). This can be a very painful period for you if your teen refuses to keep in touch, and you might be tempted to make frequent efforts to contact him. Resist this impulse, as it probably will only alienate him further.

Instead, continue to initiate opportunities for contact through a weekly phone call, perhaps with an invitation to a meal at home or at a restaurant. If he takes your call, keep your conversation casual and light. This is not the time to attempt to discuss emotionally laden issues or to give unsolicited advice. If your teen refuses phone contact, you might send him a card or note letting him know that you are there for him when he is ready to talk. You simply want him to know that you still support him emotionally even if the two of you have your differences, that your love for him continues, and that you want to keep the door open for communication.

Although this tactic usually resolves the matter, there are some teens who still refuse to move out. Even after all their money is cut off and they know that their parents can't be conned into giving them any more, somehow they keep existing off the goodwill of their friends (or a sympathetic relative who feeds them money). They may be very angry with their parents, but they dig in their heels and refuse to leave home.

If this happens at your house, you're going to have to do a very difficult thing. You'll need to give your teen a deadline and *insist* that he move out. This is a matter of "tough love," but it may not feel loving at all. In fact, you might be heavily criticized by well-meaning relatives and friends, who ask you how you can be so heartless toward your own offspring. And your teen may threaten that he'll never visit you again, accusing you of rejecting him and not caring about him.

Because it is so difficult to insist that a teen leave home, it is helpful to talk things over with a mental health professional for guidance on how to enact such a plan. He or she can help you design a reasonable strategy that is fair to all parties, as well as keep you from falling into some of the common traps that can occur while implementing it (your teen talks you into giving him money for a legitimate purpose and then spends it on something you'd not want to subsidize; he manipulates you into taking a stance that goes against what you and your spouse have previously decided). Tough Love support groups, found in many communities, can also be very helpful to parents in this situation.

The fact is that you are not helping an older teen who refuses to take responsibility by enabling him to remain dependent on you. Authentic love demands the courage to push him out of the nest when nudging him hasn't worked.

SEVEN

SEX, LOVE, AND DATING

If there's one issue that is guaranteed to bring anxiety to both parents and teens, it's sex! Beginning with the bodily changes that accompany puberty, everyone is well aware that the child of yesterday has become a sexual being.

Parents need to be able to educate their adolescent about all sexual issues candidly and without embarrassment. This includes the physical changes in the teen's body as well as issues about when to become sexually active, contraception, and sexually transmitted diseases. With some teens, the question of sexual orientation might also surface. And, of course, some teenagers will face decisions about a pregnancy.

Since dating usually begins in the teen years, parents will need to set some guidelines about when their teen will be allowed to date, and under what circumstances. Chances are high that an adolescent will fall in love at least once during the teen years, so parents need to be prepared to deal with this emotionally charged event.

PUBERTY

Ideally, you'll have prepared your teen for puberty before he or she becomes a teenager. But some issues may resurface as an anticipated (or dreaded) event becomes a reality, so chances are you'll need to discuss some of the following issues again (or to bring them up for discussion if you haven't already done so).

BODY CHANGES

You'll want to remind your teen that the age of onset of puberty is a *range* rather than a fixed age. Early-maturing girls and late-maturing boys tend to have the most anxiety about the timing of puberty, and need to be reassured that they are perfectly normal in spite of the fact that their physical maturity might seem out of sync with that of their peers.

Girls are likely to be most anxious about the size of their breasts. They need reassurance that breasts come in all shapes and sizes and that both large ones and small ones function perfectly well at the job for which they were designed: feeding babies. It's a good idea to let a girl know that it's not uncommon for adolescent girls to have a significant difference in the size of one breast compared with the other, but that the discrepancy will not affect later ability to breast-feed.

Since it's no secret that large breasts are valued by males in our society, small-breasted girls often suffer anxiety about their attractiveness to the opposite sex. On the other hand, the girl who develops unusually large breasts likewise feels self-conscious, since so much attention may be drawn to this one part of her body. Complicating her embarrassment, the well-endowed girl is often subject to totally unfounded rumors that she is sexually promiscuous.

Boys certainly do not escape anxiety about their bodies. Their primary concern is the size of their penis and the obviousness of their erections (especially the ones that spontaneously appear at totally inappropriate moments). They will read statistics about penis length and rush off to find a ruler to reassure themselves that theirs is adequate. The boy who has a small penis needs direct reassurance that both smaller and larger penises are roughly the same size when they are erect and that penis length is not associated with true masculinity.

Adolescents also become very concerned about hair distribution on their bodies. They typically scrutinize themselves, girls worrying that they may be getting too hairy (often shaving their armpits and legs) and boys worrying that they are not getting hairy enough. They also need to be reassured that it's perfectly normal to have pubic hair of a different color than the hair on their head.

MENSTRUATION

Both sexes need to know that menstruation is a normal, healthy process. Whereas bleeding is usually associated with an injury, menstrual bleeding only signals that a girl's reproductive capability is maturing. Girls will naturally want to know details about menstrual periods: when to expect them, how long they will last, and how to deal with them. They need to know that menstruation is not a debilitating condition and that they can continue with any of their normal activities. Very painful periods (as opposed to some cramping and discomfort, which can be relieved by over-the-counter pain medication) are not normal, and a girl with this problem should consult a physician.

Adults are often shocked and/or amazed at the frankness and openness among both boys and girls over the topic of menstruation. While some teens are shy about it, many girls will candidly say "I'm having my period" in front of both male and female peers. It seems that this topic has become desensitized, possibly due in part to the advertisement of feminine hygiene products on television.

Girls also need to be cautioned about an uncommon but serious infection called toxic shock syndrome, which can result from not changing one's tampon for too long a period of time. Using a fresh tampon every three to five hours, as well as using a pad instead of a tampon during sleep, is recommended as a good preventive measure.

FEMININE HYGIENE

A girl should also be instructed in good feminine hygiene. Daily bathing while she is menstruating is recommended to eliminate the possibility of unpleasant odor. She also needs to know that she will have normal vaginal secretions, which become more noticeable when she becomes sexually aroused. The moist feeling is there to provide lubrication during sexual intercourse and is no reason for concern. On the other hand, vaginal discharges that have a different color, odor, and/or produce itching are not normal and should be evaluated by a physician.

An issue that often goes unaddressed by parents, but is of great concern to a teenage girl, is the matter of female genital odor. Both boys and girls make jokes about this topic, but girls are usually too embarrassed to bring it up for discussion with a parent. Girls need to be told that all girls' and women's genitals have a characteristic odor, which is normal and is often exciting to males during lovemaking. Regular bathing and good hygiene should be all that are needed to keep any part of a girl's body fresh and clean.

THE HYMEN

If an adolescent boy or girl has not already learned about this piece of female anatomy, they are certain to hear about it when the subject of "losing one's virginity" comes up in discussion with their friends. Both sexes need to know that this thin piece of skin just inside the opening of the vagina may or may not be there *even if a girl has never had any sexual experience.*

The fact is that some girls are born without a hymen. Others have such small ones that they are hard to see. Girls can also break or stretch their hymens during vigorous exercise, such as horseback riding or gymnastics.

When a hymen is stretched or torn, whether during sexual activity or for some other reason, it *may* bleed. When it does, it might cause some mild discomfort, or it might actually hurt. But it is rare that a hymen bleeds or hurts so badly that a doctor's care is necessary.

WET DREAMS

Wet dreams, or ejaculation during sleep, are common events in most adolescent boys' lives. They are especially likely to occur if a boy is having romantic or sexual dreams. Ideally, boys need to know about wet dreams *before* experiencing them (about age twelve or thirteen) in order not to worry that something abnormal has happened when these dreams occur. They also need to know that some perfectly normal boys never have them and that a normal frequency for wet dreams can vary from hardly ever to often.

SEX EDUCATION

There is a high probability that your adolescent might become sexually active during the teen years, despite your feelings on the matter. The most recent study on sexual behavior by the Alan Guttmacher Institute reveals that only 18 percent of teenagers *do not* become sexually active at some point during the teen years; in other words, 72 percent do, usually in their middle to late teens. Consequently, it's wise to educate your teen about sexually transmitted diseases (STDs) and birth control as soon as he enters his teens, if you haven't already done so.

You might feel a great deal of conflict about discussing these issues with your adolescent, fearing that talking about them will send the message that you are giving your teen "permission" to become sexually active. To the contrary, the Guttmacher study found that programs designed to increase knowledge of sexual issues—including pregnancy and the prevention of sexually transmitted diseases—and to improve access to contraception *did not* result in participants engaging in sex earlier or more frequently than peers who were not involved in such programs, and *did not* result in higher pregnancy rates or birthrates than for nonparticipants.

However, you can be very clear about letting your teen know

your criteria for when it is appropriate for a person to become sexually active, as well as the reasons behind your beliefs. You can also acknowledge that you know your teen will make his own decision about this matter and that you want him to be informed about the risks involved in his becoming sexually active, as well as the precautions he must take to reduce these risks. Unless you have strong religious convictions to the contrary, you would probably prefer that your teen take measures to prevent pregnancy and sexually transmitted diseases should he decide to have sex.

SEXUALLY TRANSMITTED DISEASES (STDs)

With acquired immune deficiency syndrome (AIDS) a frightening reality, teens need to be given updated factual information about this disease. They need to know that AIDS is transmitted by an infected person in four ways: by sexual contact, by the sharing of needles while injecting drugs, by an infected pregnant woman to her unborn baby, and by transfusion or injection of infected blood.

Your teen needs to know that a person can be infected with the virus that causes AIDS without having any symptoms of the disease or seeming ill in any way. Even without developing the disease itself, an infected person can transmit the disease to others.

Tests have been developed to determine if the HIV virus causing AIDS and ARC (AIDS-related complex) is present in a person's blood. Someone who tests "positive" does not necessarily have AIDS and may not develop it. He or she *is*, however, a carrier whether or not (s)he develops the disease.

Tragically, we now know that many young adults who have developed AIDS contracted the HIV virus in their teen years. Moreover, current studies on high school students show a significant percentage to be HIV positive. Shockingly, many of those who know about their condition continue to be sexually active *without informing their partners*. Either due to embarrassment or, in some cases, resentment, they continue infecting unsuspecting partners. It can only be guessed how many more teens may be HIV positive but are not aware of it.

Teens need to understand clearly that even one sexual encounter can lead to death. Because of the seriousness of this possibility, sex educators stress that parents need to tell their teens the facts about STD prevention *even if* they think their teens intend to practice sexual abstinence until marriage.

There is no evidence at the time of this writing that the HIV virus is spread through casual social contact. This would include shaking hands; social kissing; coughing; sneezing; being close to or served by an infected person; or sharing a swimming pool, bed linens, eating utensils, or office equipment. Nor is it spread through the process of giving blood, as new needles are used for each donor. Whether or not AIDS can be spread through saliva (French kissing) is currently being debated, but is thought to be very unlikely.

In addition to current updated facts about AIDS, adolescents need to know about other STDs including chlamydia, gonorrhea, genital herpes, pediculosis pubis (crabs), scabies, syphilis, trichomoniasis, and venereal warts. Several of these can be extremely serious, even life-threatening. Complications can include pelvic inflammatory disease (PID) in girls, and the narrowing or blocking of the urethra and erection difficulties in boys (each of which may also result in sterility). It is particularly important for teens to know that several STDs can be contracted *without* having sexual intercourse. Herpes, syphilis, pharyngeal gonorrhea, and AIDS can be spread through oral sex.

Parents need to be frank with teens about symptoms that reflect an STD in a sexually active person. These include

- Painful, burning, or dark-colored urine
- Discharges from the vagina or penis that burn, itch, or have an unusual odor
- Soreness, sores, warts, redness, or a persistent pimple in the genital area

The best protection against STDs for both boys and girls who are sexually active is the condom. Birth control pills do not prevent acquisition of cervical gonorrhea or chlamydia, but offer significant protection (about half the risk of non–pill takers) against pelvic inflammatory disease. Spermicide and vaginal sponges (impregnated with spermicide) also offer significant protection against STDs.

The bottom line is that STDs can be avoided by practicing sexual abstinence, or by having a mutually monogamous marriage or relationship with an uninfected person. Obviously, having multiple sex partners greatly increases the risk of acquiring STDs.

If information about "safer sex" is presented to teenagers in a calm, knowledgeable manner, they are more likely to take it seriously. Also, the discussion may be the very thing to convince an adolescent to practice abstinence for a longer period of time.

CONTRACEPTION

Although parents need to make very clear the circumstances under which they consider it appropriate for a person to have sexual relations, they also need to point out the importance of sexual responsibility once that person begins a sexual relationship, whether married or otherwise. Protecting oneself and/or one's partner from conceiving an unwanted child and/or contracting a sexually transmitted disease is part of such responsibility.

Clearly, you'll need to let your teenager know that the only foolproof method of contraception is abstinence. However, many teens elect to become sexually active before a parent would approve, so they need to be aware that there are several methods of birth control with varying degrees of protection against pregnancy.

The most reliable forms of birth control (the pill and the diaphragm) are used by a female and can be obtained only after an examination by a physician. Vaginal sponges, chemical contraceptives (foams, jellies, suppositories, and creams) and condoms (rubbers) can all be purchased over the counter in a drugstore or supermarket. All of the above methods must be used conscientiously *every time* a sexual encounter occurs.

Couples who disapprove of mechanical or chemical means of contraception due to religious reasons can use the "rhythm method," also known as natural family planning (NFP). This system relies on a girl's careful charting of her menstrual cycle and of her daily temperature and condition of her vaginal mucous in order to determine the time of ovulation. These charts must be kept for *several months* in order to establish the girl's cycle, and this method is thought to be highly unreliable, even in adults, because of poor compliance. Obviously, NFP offers no protection against STDs.

In practice, the contraceptive methods thought to be most preferred by teenagers are the pill and the condom. Other methods tend to be too cumbersome, awkward, or messy. The condom requires more planning than the pill; it also requires proper application and use in order to be effective. Experts recommend using a condom *in addition* to any other method of birth control in order to prevent the transmission of STDs.

Teens can also be told about the postcoital contraceptive ("morning-after pill"). It requires a doctor's prescription, but it is quite reliable if taken within seventy-two hours of unprotected, midcycle coitus. Most authorities view the method as suitable for emergency situations (rape, broken condom) rather than for regular use. Parents need to stress that this method is *not* to be regarded as a form of contraception.

Boys should be cautioned that they should not take a girl at her word if she tells them that she is on the pill or that she can't get pregnant for some other reason. It's not that the girl is necessarily lying (although she may be), but that she may have an unconscious wish to become pregnant. She may also not have taken her pills conscientiously, as is often the case with teenage girls, or she may simply have a very irregular menstrual cycle. Also, a boy needs to use a condom to prevent both partners from acquiring an STD.

Both boys and girls need to know that a menstrual cycle is not a very accurate way of calculating periods of fertility, especially in the teen years, when a girl's cycle may be very irregular. Also, girls do sometimes ovulate more than once a month, and it is possible, though rare, for a teen to become pregnant while menstruating.

Unfortunately, even teens who have been well informed about contraception may not use it. To see a doctor for this purpose or to purchase contraceptives requires admitting to oneself that one is planning to have sex. Many teens do not want to admit that this is what they are planning; they would rather blame their sexual activity on an argument with a parent, the pressure of exams, a bad day, an especially romantic occasion, or some other external force.

It is helpful for parents to point this out to teens, encouraging them to see that facing up to their true intentions is a sign of maturity. Parents can also make it clear that having sex is *never* an emergency (even though it might feel that way to a teen) and that an all-night drugstore or supermarket can almost always be found to purchase contraceptives.

Although you can encourage your teenager to come to you for assistance in obtaining birth control if she does become sexually active during adolescence, you also need to make her aware that doctors can prescribe contraceptives *without* parental knowledge or consent. In this way, your teen can be reassured that she can still obtain birth control from a private physician or a community clinic even if she does not wish to confide in you.

It's also wise to remind your teen that "heavy petting" and mutual masturbation are ways of expressing sexual feelings with a partner without adding the complications and physical/emotional risks involved in having sexual intercourse. Be sure to caution her, however, about the fact that preejaculatory fluid and/or semen ejaculated near the vagina although not in it can still result in a girl's becoming pregnant, and that oral sex can transmit STDs.

HOW TO TALK ABOUT SEXUAL ISSUES

While you might want to have open discussion with your teen about the physical and emotional aspects of sexuality, you might be uncertain about how to bring up these subjects with him or her, or even what exactly to say once you do bring them up. After all, many parents of today's teenagers grew up in homes where such matters were not discussed, or if they were, they were talked about with an aura of shame or secrecy. Without good role models, many parents feel very awkward when they discuss sexual topics with their adolescents.

If you approach your teen with "I was wondering if you have any questions about sex?" chances are your adolescent will have a somewhat amused look on his face as he quickly reassures you that he has none. This answer probably means that he doesn't want to admit that he is uninformed, or that he feels embarrassed talking about such matters with, God forbid, a parent. So don't fall for the "I already know all that stuff" ploy.

Instead, take advantage of natural opportunities when a sexual issue is brought up by your teen, by someone else, or even by a television show. Examples would include a discussion on birth control when the subject of a pregnant teen comes up, on feminine hygiene when a commercial about it appears on television, on STDs when AIDS is talked about. You can also use movies and television shows to educate your teen about the realities of sexuality by pointing out the many unrealistic aspects of media sex (people being "swept away" with passion without mention of sexual history, STDs, or birth control).

It is also very helpful to give your adolescent a book about puberty, if you haven't done so already. You can casually introduce it by saying something like "I know you probably know most of this stuff, but I thought you might like to have this to refer to if needed." You can also add a comment that "If you have any questions after you've looked it over, let me know and we'll talk about it, okay?" If you want, you can add a particular emphasis by stating, "I think the chapter on AIDS is really great," or "Boy, I wish somebody had given me this information on masturbation when I was your age." Even though your teen might give you a scornful look when you hand him the book, it's very likely that he'll be curious about its contents once he's alone.

If you are a parent who has been very embarrassed and uncomfortable about discussing sex, you might tell this fact to your teen (he probably senses it anyway). But you can break the ice by saying, "You know, Brad, I've never been very comfortable talking about sexual things when you were younger, but I want you to know that you can feel free to come to me with any questions you have about it now. I could never talk to my dad about sex, but I want it to be different between us. Is there anything on your mind that you'd like to talk over?"

Remember that you don't have to wait for your teen to raise the questions; you can ask him his opinion of specific topics. For example, "What do you think about kids who are having sex without condoms?" "Have you ever wondered how a boy knows if he might have a sexually transmitted disease?" "Is there a lot of pressure in your school for teens to have sex?" Obviously, such questions need to be brought up in a context where the topic has been introduced so that your questions do not seem "off the wall" to your adolescent.

SEXUAL ORIENTATION

While a person's sexual orientation is thought to be established between ages three and ten, it is in adolescence that it reaches full expression. Usually, this means a heterosexual orientation, which is why relationships with the opposite sex generally become so important in a teen's life. But not always.

Adolescence is also the time when youngsters may express a preference for bisexuality or homosexuality. Parents are typically anguished by these choices, since many people consider such sexual orientations to be deviant, or at least much less desirable than a heterosexual one. Even parents who are homosexuals usually prefer their children to be heterosexual due to the realistic problems and prejudices a gay person of either sex faces in our society. Consequently, a parent's suspicion or discovery that a teen is gay or bisexual can cause feelings of disbelief, anxiety, guilt, shame, anger, and/or disgust.

It's important both for parents and teens to understand that many "normal" heterosexual men and women report having had one or several sexual contacts with people of the same sex, especially during their childhood or adolescence. Young adolescent boys, in particular, may engage in group sex play that is best viewed as experimentation rather than as a critical factor in later sexual behavior. Teens who have experimented with any kind of same-sex contact, whether they initiated it or were seduced by the other individual, may leap to the false conclusion that they are homosexual and always will be. The truth is that same-sex experimentation can be just a part of growing up for some teens. Helping them to know this can alleviate much unnecessary anxiety about this sensitive issue.

Obviously, some teens do become homosexual or bisexual. If this is true of your adolescent, it may be of some comfort to know that research has not borne out any particular pattern of parenting that results in homosexuality for males or females. Instead, two factors have been identified that may explain the development of homosexuality. The first has to do with hormonal differences that are thought to exist from birth; the second with a kind of imprinting that can occur when a youngster of any age is strongly or repeatedly sexually aroused through seduction by someone of the same sex. Since most of us have our "sexual awakening" with a partner of the opposite sex, most of us become heterosexual.

There are also some teens whose homosexual behavior is a result of trauma with the opposite sex rather than a genuine emotional preference. An example is the girl who is aggressively molested by a male and decides, perhaps unconsciously, that she will only allow herself to be sexual with females. If she is able in psychotherapy to work through the original trauma, she may decide that her true preference is heterosexuality.

DATE RAPE

Unfortunately, a problem that is affecting our teenagers more and more in today's world is date rape. Consequently, girls need to know how to protect themselves against it, and boys need to know how to protect themselves from being accused of it.

Begin educating your teen in early adolescence about this important subject. Teach your daughter that there is a difference between innocent flirting and "coming on" to a boy. She should never give a boy mixed messages about sex; for example, she should not tease him when he's being romantic by coquettishly telling him no when she really wants him to go farther. If she says no without really meaning it, she leads him to expect that no doesn't, in fact, mean no. When she really does mean no, he's not likely to take her seriously. Let her know that even if she's agreed to some sexual activity, she *always* has the right to change her mind. If this happens, her no should be forceful and convincing, not said weakly or ambivalently.

Teach your son that he should always respect a girl's saying no to a sexual advance, even if he's not sure she really means it. Let him know that girls sometimes agree to sexual activities and then change their minds. Just because she's agreed to something he's suggested, he should stop immediately if she changes her mind, or even seems reluctant.

Caution your teen that heavy petting can lead to feelings of physical urgency that are difficult to control. Both sexes need to be aware of this fact, because judgment can easily be suspended in the heat of passion. Also, teens need to know that alcohol and drugs can seriously affect a person's judgment. Girls need to know that drinking alcohol can leave them vulnerable to a boy's sexual advances and that some boys will deliberately take sexual advantage of such a situation. Both boys and girls should be fully emotionally engaged—not influenced by alcohol or drugs—if and when they have sex.

THE LEGAL SIDE

Many teens (and parents) remain very uninformed about the degree of legal trouble a teen can encounter because of sexual behavior, or the *accusation* of it. For example, adults may have an understanding of the concept of statutory rape, yet be ignorant about exactly what constitutes it; teens might not even know about the concept. Yet every state has laws that make it illegal and punishable for a male to have sex with an "underage" female. The problem is each state is different in its determination of what is underage, as well as in what the punishment should be. For example, some states prosecute a male for committing statutory rape if he has had sexual intercourse with a female who is under seventeen and who is *more than two years younger* than he. A teenage boy needs to know the laws for his particular state and to realize that an "underage" girl who *consents* to have sex with him may have a parent who does not consent and who may press charges upon finding out that he has been sexual with their daughter.

Teenagers also need to know about third-degree sexual assault. This term refers to a boy (usually) who touches the breasts or genitals of a girl (*even over her clothes*) when the girl has asked him to stop. This is considered an assault *even if* the boy and girl have had a petting relationship.

The *consequences* of third-degree sexual assault are often a shock to both parents and teens. They commonly include a court trial or a plea bargain with two years' probation. In addition to the legal expenses involved for the family, the teen is placed on a "sexual offender" list in any city he lives until he's twenty-one years old. Other consequences include not being allowed to work with young people at day care or camps and having to report to a local agency if traveling to another state. In many states, any further charge of sexual misconduct automatically results in imprisonment; consequently, the offender has to be extremely careful not to put himself in a potentially compromising situation. Often this means being advised by the probation officer not to put himself in situations where other people are not present to witness his interaction with the opposite sex (for example, going jogging with a girl without others present).

Unfortunately, information about third-degree sexual assault is currently not common knowledge. Young adolescent boys, who are often very casual and impulsive about sexual touching, are quite vulnerable to these serious legal repercussions.

Of course, any legal proceeding involving sexual misconduct (rape, date rape, or sexual assault) often involves one person's word against another's. Proving or disproving an accusation can be very difficult, and decisions made by judges and juries often have more to do with the lawyers' abilities and/or the seeming credibility of the two parties, making it a risky venture for either the accuser or the accusee.

COMMON DILEMMAS

MASTURBATION

Thinking nobody else is home, you walk into the bathroom to put away a load of clean towels. You're shocked to find fourteen-year-old Alex looking at a girlie magazine and masturbating.

Tell your son something like "Sorry. I didn't know you were in here," and leave the bathroom. No doubt, both you and your son will need a chance to collect yourselves. Realize that masturbation is a perfectly normal event in the life of a teenager (boy or girl) and should be no cause for concern, unless, of course, you have religious beliefs that prohibit its practice. In fact, the only common psychological problem associated with masturbation is the guilt that results *if* a person has been taught to believe that masturbation is unnatural or deviant.

Whether or not you discuss the incident with your son will be an individual matter. It is to be hoped that before your son entered adolescence, you dispelled those myths about masturbation leading to hair on the palms, insanity, and other such ridiculous claims. But if you haven't, you might want to take advantage of the opportunity provided by your bathroom intrusion and dispel any guilt your son might be feeling.

Obviously, you'll want to be sensitive to your son's embarrassment about getting caught and not make a big deal out of the matter. You might say something like "I'm really sorry I walked in on you in the bathroom this afternoon. That's not exactly a time when a person wants an audience!" This message implies that your teen has done nothing wrong and that his activity was a private affair.

If you are a father, you might also say something about the fact that you were really embarrassed as a teen when someone caught you (or almost caught you) masturbating. Such a statement implies that your teen's activity is a normal male event. Likewise, if you are a mother and have walked in on your daughter when she's masturbating, you could let her know that you're not a prude, that you have masturbated before (if true), and that she doesn't have to be upset about the fact that you know she is doing it.

Even if you feel nonchalant about masturbation, you might be concerned if you think that your teen is masturbating excessively. Perhaps he spends a long time in the bathroom every evening, and you suspect that masturbation might be the reason for it.

Teenagers, especially boys, are known to have a high level of sexual drive and may masturbate daily, perhaps even several times a day. Whether this is excessive depends on what else is going on in the teen's life. If he has friends, normal activities and interests, and spends some time interacting with other people (family or friends), his masturbation isn't interfering with the rest of his life. On the other hand, if he's very isolated and seems preoccupied with masturbation, consultation with a mental health professional is suggested.

PREMARITAL SEX

You and fourteen-year-old Trisha are watching a television program in which a teenage girl is telling a peer that she is having sex with her boyfriend. At the end of the program, your daughter asks, "Do you believe it's okay to have sex when you're not married?"

Obviously, your answer is going to depend heavily on your own personal value system. If you are a firm believer that people should remain abstinent until they are married, then say so. You're likely to have more of a problem knowing what to say if you believe that premarital sex is okay, or even desirable, because you would probably want to qualify this answer with several conditions. It is highly unlikely that any parent would want his or her teen to be promiscuous or to engage in casual sexual encounters. Also, the age at which your teen becomes sexually active is probably less important than the circumstances under which it occurs. Most parents hope that their offspring's first sexual experience, married or not, will occur in a context of mutual love, commitment, safety, and responsibility.

Obviously, there is a strong tradition in this country that supports a belief in abstinence until marriage. The reality of AIDS and other sexually transmitted diseases, and the risk of unwanted pregnancy, are strong arguments for the abstinence position.

Even if you take the traditional stance that sex should wait until marriage, however, realize that each person's decision to be sexual is essentially his or her own responsibility, out of parental control. Your teen may decide to become sexually active long before ever thinking of marriage, with or without your approval.

Because of this fact, it's wise to let your teenager know that you are well aware that there is a great deal of pressure on teens to have sex and that many teenagers do so without being married. Let her know that if she should decide to reject your ideas about saving sex for marriage, she needs to think through very carefully her *own* criteria about when it is appropriate to be sexual. Likewise, if you believe that premarital sex is all right, you'll want your teen to consider the conditions under which it would be acceptable.

A good place to start when you discuss such criteria is to specify the necessary ingredients for a successful and mature sexual relationship. Let her know that trust and commitment are paramount and that a couple cannot possibly know about these qualities in each other unless they have dated steadily for a significant length of time. She needs to know that it takes *time* before the newness of "putting one's best foot forward" wears off, before a couple has a chance to see how each other acts when they disagree, and to be reasonably sure that a partner is consistently thoughtful, considerate, and truthful.

Your teen also needs to understand that boys and girls typically have sex for *different* reasons. An adolescent boy is more likely to be sexual to gain experience, make a conquest, bolster his feelings of masculinity, feel more grown up, or to be able to brag to his friends about his sexual experiences. Adolescent girls, on the other hand, are likely to view sex as an expression of love. They are much less likely to be consciously having sex to impress their girlfriends or to gain expertise!

Obviously, a girl is most sexually vulnerable if a boy is able to convince her that he is "in love" with her. Boys, of course, quickly figure this out and use it to their advantage. Consequently, your daughter needs to know that in the heat of passion (or even without passion), a boy might promise *anything* in order to talk a girl into being sexual with him. This has nothing to do with mature love, although he may tell her that he loves her, even sincerely.

Another criterion for a positive sexual experience has to do with physical safety and comfort. Having a furtive grope session in the backseat of a car, hoping not to be discovered or mugged, leaves much to be desired on both counts.

Certainly, you'll want to bring into this discussion of criteria the matter of sexual responsibility. This is a good time to find out what your teen knows about sexually transmitted diseases and to give her information about them. This is also the time to talk about birth control and to ask your daughter to consider the moral and practical dilemmas faced by a teen couple who unintentionally conceive a baby.

Be sure to point out to your adolescent that many emotional complications surface once sex enters a relationship. Teens who might want to date someone else can feel constrained by the sexual ties to a partner. Also, it takes maturity to be able to assess the character of a partner, and many teens discover *with hindsight* that the person they had sex with was exploitative and/or unfaithful. The majority of teenage romances do end, and a breakup can be even more painful when a couple has experienced the special closeness of sexual intimacy.

Finally, ask your teen to estimate how many boyfriends/girlfriends the average girl or boy is likely to have during the teen years. For example, if a girl has three or four boyfriends a year beginning at age fourteen, by the time she's twenty-one, she would have had roughly twenty-one to twenty-eight boyfriends. If she had believed she was in love with each one at the time they were dating, and if she had been sexual with every boy whom she loved, think how many sexual partners she might have had by the time she becomes an adult! Most teens are quite surprised when the number is calculated and realize that it represents a large number of sexual partners to have had upon entering adulthood. It also gives you an opportunity to drive home the point about the correlation between multiple sexual partners and the likelihood of contracting an STD.

Be sure to let your adolescent know that there are other alternatives besides sexual intercourse for releasing those normal sexual urges. Masturbation is a healthy outlet and has the obvious advantage of being an excellent form of "safe sex" (if you have no religious prohibitions against it). Also, heavy petting is a way to be sexual with a partner without adding the complications and risks involved in having sexual intercourse; however, teens need to be cautioned that such petting is risky in itself due to the willpower that is often necessary to resist the temptations it presents.

A BAD REPUTATION

One of your worst fears has come true—your sixteen-year-old daughter, Deidre, is getting a reputation for sexual promiscuity. It seems that she's been casually sleeping around, and you're shocked and heartbroken.

It is a fact that the double standard is still alive and well in our society. Boys can have casual sex and be thought of as "gaining experience" or "sowing their wild oats"; girls who do the same thing are labeled sluts. Interestingly, boys who are promiscuous in their teens do not necessarily have low self-esteem or other emotional problems; promiscuous girls, however, typically have both.

If you discover that your daughter is in this position, you'll want to let her know that you are aware of her sexual behavior and are very concerned about it. Sometimes just bringing the matter out in the open results in a girl's confession that she has been raped or sexually abused, either recently or in her childhood. Female victims of such abuse often don't tell anyone about the incident(s), but feel guilty and responsible for what happened to them. The demise of their self-esteem takes its toll and may be reflected in such self-destructive behavior such as sexual promiscuity. Consequently, if a teen begins to engage in casual sex, it's important to ask her specifically about the possibility of sexual abuse.

Whether or not abuse is the cause of her behavior, consultation with a mental health professional is recommended to gain understanding about why a teen is engaging in sexual acting out, and to help her change this behavior. Is she succumbing to peer pressure from a particular group? Is she angry about some family issue, and her behavior represents rebellion? Is she feeling neglected and is trying to get pregnant in order to have "someone to love"? Is she involved in drug or alcohol abuse and is getting into sexual situations through such involvement?

In spite of your strong feelings about your daughter's dangerous behavior, you need to remain emotionally supportive toward her. Rather than telling her she's ruined her life, you need to give her the positive encouragement that you know she will work through whatever problems are creating this situation and that you are there to help her. She needs to know that you love and care for her even though you strongly disapprove of her behavior and that you will get her the professional help she needs to heal her emotional troubles.

Of course, you'll also need to help your daughter deal with the reality of having developed a bad reputation, which can follow her throughout her high school years. For this reason many girls in this situation choose to change their environment, going to a different school and becoming involved with a new group of peers. Such a change is not always possible, however. If this is the case, you can encourage your daughter by reminding her that eventually it will become obvious that she has changed, and her reputation will be updated. In the meantime, she can involve herself in activities, both in and out of school, that will help her develop new friends and interests.

POOR TREATMENT OF A GIRLFRIEND

Seventeen-year-old Charlie clearly is not treating his girlfriend well. The two supposedly are seeing each other exclusively, but your son is cheating on her.

While your son might react by telling you to "mind your own business," it's important that you find an opportunity to confront him about his behavior. Pick a time when neither of you is upset and you won't be disturbed (taking him out for a meal creates a captive audience!). Tell him that you're concerned about his relationship with his girlfriend and ask if he's experiencing problems with her. This approach gives him an opportunity to open up to you about any ambivalence he might feel toward his commitment to this girl. If he doesn't bring up any problems, let him know that you asked the question because you're aware that he's been deceiving her and that you don't consider that a good relationship strategy.

In the course of your conversation, you'll want to let him know that deceit breeds resentment and mistrust. Suggest that he's likely not to be ready for a serious commitment if he wants to see other girls and that there's nothing wrong with his not wanting to tie himself to one girl. The problem is that he needs to be truthful with her about this. While an honest discussion will hurt her feelings, as all rejection does, it is far more hurtful in the long run to deceive her. If he truly cares for her, he'll want to be mature enough to tell her that he's just not ready for a heavy commitment; in this way, he's not teaching her to distrust men.

Although you might express your views about this topic in the best possible manner, your son still might continue his behavior. Remember that many adults have the same difficulty extricating themselves from relationships, and that it takes a great deal of maturity to handle these situations responsibly. Teens are beginning to learn about relationships, and sometimes they learn their lessons the hard way. As is true with many issues, you can clearly let your teen know how you feel, but you cannot control his behavior.

DATING RULES

Sixteen-year-old Melanie is all decked out to go to a school dance. She tells you that she's meeting her date at a restaurant, as they plan to eat dinner before going to the dance. You've never met her date, and you find out that your daughter first met him just that week at the mall!

As much as your teen might try to convince you otherwise, boys do still meet a girl's parents before taking her out on a date, and they still pick up their dates at the girl's home—that is, *if* a parent insists on it.

The time to establish rules about going out with the opposite sex is when your teen first begins to date. Usually the ground rules stipulate that a parent must have met the boy, and if he's someone the girl met by chance (rather than a schoolmate, a friend's brother, a peer in the church youth group, and so on), he must come to the house a few times *before* the girl is allowed to go out with him alone. You'll probably also want the boy to bring your daughter home after a date rather than having her drive herself home or allowing her to be dropped off by someone else.

While not foolproof, this system at least gives some minimal assurance that the boy your daughter wants to date is an okay guy. Boys who refuse to met a girl's parents, or to pick her up and bring her home, are often bad news. You'll want your daughter to understand this principle right from the start of her dating career.

Certainly there are times when a girl might drive to a boy's house to pick him up, or meet him at an agreed-upon location. Likewise, there are times when she might not have a date accompany her home. But these situations should happen after a dating relationship has been established, not in the initial phase.

If your teen is on her way to meet someone you've never met, as in the situation above, you could insist that she not go. A practical compromise might be to give her the option either of not going on the date or of taking a friend with her throughout the evening and allowing the mysterious boy to provide his own transportation to and from the dance.

DATING "OLDER" BOYS

Sixteen-year-old Melody has had a few dates with Max, who seems polite and courteous when he comes to pick her up. In fact, you admire the fact that Max is working as a waiter while he's in school. Then the bomb drops: You find out that Max is twenty-two and a senior in college!

The obvious question becomes "Why would a twenty-two-year-old man want to date a sixteen-year-old girl?" Even if his intentions are the best, why would he put up with the rules and constraints that most sixteen-year-old girls are given by their parents? After all, a college girl probably would not have a curfew, could visit him in his dorm or apartment, could go to some nightclubs, and wouldn't have to answer to parents!

As sensible as all this sound to you, it's not likely to convince your daughter that she shouldn't be dating someone older. She's likely to accuse you of being old-fashioned and bigoted (against guys who are older), and of insulting her level of maturity, if you insist that she not date this man.

To strengthen your message about this situation, invite the young man for a meeting with you and your spouse. Tell him your concerns about his wanting to date a sixteen-year-old and that you feel it is inappropriate. Let him know that, while you have nothing against him personally, you will not allow your daughter to see him. Make it clear that you expect him to abide by your wishes and that you do not want him contacting your daughter.

You may be afraid to take such a hard line, fearing that your daughter might do something foolishly rebellious, such as running off with this man. Although this is a *possibility*, you would have legal recourse if this actually happened (since he is an adult and she is a minor). Realize that teens in the heat of an emotional discussion will often make threats that they never carry out. If you give in to this kind of manipulation, you have lost parental control. If your teen *should* carry through on the threat, you'll simply have to deal with it.

What *is* likely to happen is that your adolescent will be very angry with you. However, it can be amazing to see how quickly a teen will settle back into a normal routine after an initial angry outburst. Usually, when a parent is crystal clear about a position, with no wavering, a teen is able to accept it and to move on.

IN LOVE

Seventeen-year-old Chuck is head over heels in love with a girl whom you consider to be a totally inappropriate match. You think she is possessive, controlling, and immature. Besides that, she practices a very different religion from yours. You're worried that your son is getting too serious with her, and wonder what you might do to discourage their relationship.

Unfortunately, your trying to break up the couple will probably only strengthen their relationship and may alienate your teen from you in the process. A parent who goes so far as to forbid an older teen's relationship usually only invites rebellion, sometimes driving the couple into a premature marriage.

Likewise, if you let your son know that you are displeased with his choice, he'll probably become very defensive about the girl. He will give an excuse or a counterexample to everything negative you point out about her, even if he inwardly agrees with your comment. In trying to drive them apart, you'll usually end up pushing them closer together.

Many parents try to convince an adolescent that he's really not in love, that he doesn't know what love is, or that he's experiencing "puppy love." Such comments will only polarize your teen to your position, in addition to making him feel that you are discounting his feelings and have no understanding. While his judgment may be poor, his feelings of love are genuine. True, he may not be experiencing what you define as *mature* love, but realize that he has nothing with which to compare his feelings. At twenty-five, or forty, he might look back and consider his love for his high-school sweetheart as immature, but he can't possibly make that distinction now.

The best tactic is to remain neutral and matter-of-fact when you talk about the girlfriend. You can express your concerns about her when your son is in a receptive mood, such as one of those times when neither of you is mad at the other and he brings up something about the relationship. Rather than making direct statements reflecting your disapproval ("How can you even think of getting serious with someone who's not of our faith?" "Don't you see how she's just leading you around like a dog on a leash?"), ask your teen questions ("Do you worry sometimes about the differences in your religions?" "Do you think she considers your wishes as much as you consider hers?"), or make objective rather than emotional comments ("I'm concerned about your getting so serious with a girl who's not of our faith because couples who have very different religions can find it hard to continue their own religious practices, especially when kids come along"; "I get the impression that she usually gets her way, and I imagine you must get pretty angry with her about that").

It is true that this kind of objective stance will not *guarantee* that your teen won't continue the relationship. However, given enough time, the chance is high that the relationship will break up, especially in those years right after graduation from high school. If you let nature take its course, your son is likely to see the problems in his current relationship much sooner than if you try to over-influence him at this point. Your focus needs to be on getting your son to postpone marrying *anyone* in the next few years rather than on breaking up this particular relationship.

FINDING EVIDENCE OF BIRTH CONTROL

Seventeen-year-old Kimberly accidentally spills the contents of her purse onto the floor. To your complete shock, out falls a container of birth control pills that bears her name on the prescription label on the front of it!

No doubt you'll feel very upset by this turn of events, especially if you've raised your daughter to value abstinence until marriage. You may feel betrayed, angry, and hurt to realize that she is sexually active.

Difficult as it can be, realize that there is nothing you can do at this point to erase the fact that your daughter is having sex. The more rational side of you must recognize that even though your teen has done something you very much disapprove of, at least she has been responsible about it. You'll probably agree that finding out your teen is pregnant would be much worse.

Your daughter, of course, hid from you the fact that she is on birth control pills because she knew you would disapprove. She obviously felt that she couldn't come to you and tell you that she is sexually active. If you had advised her to tell you if she ever became sexually active so that you could take her to a physician to explore birth control options, you might feel even more hurt that she didn't confide in you.

While you may be very disappointed that your daughter is sexually active and/or that she didn't talk with you about it, you'll need to distinguish between being disappointed with her *decision* and being disappointed with *her*. Some parents say things like "I'm so disappointed in you," creating in the girl potentially lasting feelings of shame, guilt, and even unworthiness.

At this point, your focus needs to be on exploring her reasons for becoming sexually active. If she has a steady boyfriend and you know the two are in love, the reason is obvious. But what if she doesn't? Wait until the two of you have gotten over the initial shock of your discovery and then have a heart-to-heart talk with your daughter about her decision to be sexually active. You'll want to get her to focus on her *criteria* for having sex with someone, hoping that your discussion will help her to set strong standards in the future. If she's having casual sex, you'll be concerned about her self-esteem, about whether or not she's been sexually abused, about her vulnerability to peer pressure. Admit that this is a difficult topic to discuss with one's parent and ask if she would like to consult with a professional about her situation.

When the subject is sex, many parents want their teens to talk things over with a priest, minister, or rabbi. If your teen is actively involved with spiritual worship, or receptive to it, this can be an excellent choice. However, if your teen is turned off at the idea of seeing someone whose emphasis is religious, forcing her to see such a person will only set her up to sabotage the counseling process. In such a case, ask her to talk things over with a mental health professional.

HOMOSEXUALITY

You are encouraging seventeen-year-old Kelvin to get a date for the school prom. Suddenly, he bursts into tears and tells you that he is gay.

The teen who is, or who thinks he might be, homosexual usually goes through a painful process of accepting his sexual orientation. He may feel guilty or ashamed, and often is most terrified by a fear that he will lose the love of his parents and family if he discloses his true feelings. When he does confide in them, he needs a parent's support rather than rejection.

Difficult as it might be for you to hear your son's confession, keep your own emotions in check and treat him with compassion. Acknowledge that it must have been very difficult for him to tell you this, and that, no matter what, you will always love him. Rather than protesting, analyzing, disbelieving, lecturing, or exploding, simply encourage your son to tell you what has led him to conclude that he is gay.

If your son has reached his conclusion because he's had one or two experiences with someone of the same sex, let him know that this fact doesn't necessarily mean that he's gay. Many heterosexuals have experimented with homosexual behavior, especially in adolescence. Although you give him this reassurance, refrain from acting as if you are trying to talk him out of being gay. He may be, and your goal is to let him know that this is a complicated issue, and that you want him to get more information about his sexuality.

Admit your ignorance about the issue, and ask him to see a mental health professional to get an objective opinion. If you ask him to see a counselor so that he can *change* his preference, he may have no interest in doing so; in this case, you'll only alienate him and reduce the likelihood that he will accept your suggestion for therapy.

Realize that while it can be helpful for a teen who is engaging in homosexual behavior or fantasies to consult a therapist, you cannot expect that the counseling will necessarily change your teen's sexual orientation. Even homosexual men and women who clearly want to become heterosexual have varying degrees of success in doing so. Therapy can help a teen discover whether, in fact, he has a basis to think he's gay and, if so, to determine his options about it. The therapist will explore the possibility of sexual trauma or molestation, the strength of heterosexual fantasies and behavior, if present, and the degree of the teen's motivation to change his sexual preference.

If your teen is, in fact, homosexual or bisexual, realize that he'll have difficulty having high self-esteem if he is made to feel ashamed of his sexuality. As with a heterosexual teen, a parent's emphasis needs to focus on sexuality as a channel for the expression of loving and caring between two individuals.

Remember, there is no parenting pattern that has been found to "cause" homosexuality. This fact can greatly assuage any feelings of guilt you might have about your teen's sexual orientation.

PREGNANCY

Seventeen-year-old Michelle asks to speak with you privately. As you enter her room, you can tell she's upset. Then she tearfully confesses that she's pregnant.

While you may feel heartbroken and/or angry, a pregnancy is a *fait accompli.* Your daughter is probably feeling frightened, confused, embarrassed, guilty, and generally upset. Your job at this point is to give her support, love, and objective help in facing the realities of her situation, not to lecture her about why she shouldn't have gotten pregnant in the first place. Of course, you are going through your own emotional crisis. But you are the parent, and your first priority needs to be to help your daughter face *her* emotional crisis.

Obviously, you'll want to start by asking your daughter how she knows that she's pregnant. It may be that she only *thinks* this is true because of a missed menstrual period, because she's been feeling nauseated in the mornings, or because of the presence of some other symptom that may accompany a pregnancy. Insist that she get a pregnancy test ordered by a physician immediately, even if she's taken a home pregnancy test (because this could be inaccurate).

Examination by a physician is recommended if she is pregnant in order to determine how advanced the pregnancy is and other factors that might need to be evaluated. These might include your daughter's general state of health, physical anomalies of her reproductive system, and any illness she may have experienced or medication she may have taken since her pregnancy began. Taking all these things into consideration, the doctor will be able to advise you and your daughter about the probability of her delivering a healthy baby.

If your teen is, in fact, pregnant, she has three options: having the baby and keeping it, having the baby and giving it up for adoption, and abortion. You may have very strong opinions about which option your daughter should pursue, but it is very important that the decision be *hers* if she is mentally competent and in her mid-to-late teens. Even a younger teen needs to take part in making this important decision, as she will be the one to live with the consequences.

Girls who are pushed into any one of the three options without being given a chance to figure out what *they* think is best can suffer tremendous emotional consequences, including being very angry with the person who forced the decision on them. Although you may want your daughter to know your preference and the reasons for it, you'll be helping her immensely by giving her permission to make the decision she thinks is best for her.

If you are too emotional about the situation, or if you find that you cannot be objective due to your own strong bias, let your daughter see a counselor in order to explore her options. Otherwise, you can assist her by discussing each option in detail, encouraging her to gather facts along the way that can help her make an informed decision. For example, if she's going to have the baby, her decision to keep it versus giving it up for adoption can be better made after she's looked into the kinds of adoptions that are possible (open versus traditional), as well as finding out the cost of food, supplies, child care, and other expenses she'll have if she chooses to keep her baby. You'll also want to help her think about how she'll handle the everyday realities of having a baby, including her plans for school, work, and so on. Is someone willing to help her take care of her baby, or will it be her total financial and physical responsibility?

If your daughter is considering abortion, she'll need information from a physician about how one is done. Procedures can vary according to the length of the pregnancy, and a decision to abort has to be made within a certain time frame, or it will be too late to terminate the pregnancy under legal guidelines. Girls have different emotional reactions to having an abortion. Some do not experience emotional distress, some feel guilty but are able to forgive themselves and find peace, and some suffer continuing emotional distress about their decision.

Of course, it takes two to make a baby, and your daughter's relationship with the baby's father may well play a part in her decision about the pregnancy. Some boys take this responsibility seriously, and some don't. The couple may want to marry, although this probably should be discouraged unless the relationship has been a long and healthy one. Fortunately, girls today do not have to feel compelled to marry just because they are pregnant, even if the fathers will play an active role in the baby's upbringing.

Make sure that your daughter understands that although the father's opinions and feelings need to be heard, she does not have to be pushed into making the decision that he wants if she is not comfortable with it. She will be the one having the baby and probably the one raising it, or she will be the one having the abortion. The final decision needs to be one that she makes, given her best intentions and judgment.

Of course, many males in such a situation feel quite helpless about the fact that a pregnant female has the ultimate power in making a decision about whether or not a pregnancy is terminated. However, if the girl decides to have the baby, the father does have legal say-so about whether or not the child can be put up for adoption.

Remember, also, that a teen pregnancy can result in a potential grandchild, and the teen mother's or father's parents can have very strong feelings about the matter. Many parents of teens struggle with the utter lack of control they have in such a situation and may truly grieve the loss of their grandchild if that child is given up for adoption.

The other issue to address—right away if she chooses abortion, later on if she has the baby—is birth control. She and her physician can best decide what form of contraception will be most suitable for her. However, some parents, especially if the pregnancy has been terminated, still do not want their daughter to consider birth control measures. The girl may promise that she has learned a lesson and that she will remain abstinent until marriage.

Unfortunately, even if she is sincere in her assertions, statistics tell us that most girls who have been sexually active will continue to be so, even after an unwanted pregnancy. They may think they'll remain abstinent, but this decision made shortly on the heels of a pregnancy can easily change once they enter into another relationship. Consequently, the safer—and less naive—option is to encourage a girl to practice birth control after a pregnancy. If her intentions to remain abstinent hold, she can still continue to practice celibacy even if she is on birth control pills or has access to other forms of birth control.

Once again, take the opportunity provided by an unwanted pregnancy to help your daughter reevaluate her criteria for being sexual with someone. Perhaps she will be amenable to deciding to become abstinent until marriage, or at least until she's older. But be sure she realizes that even girls who conscientiously practice birth control get pregnant. If she's going to remain sexually active, encourage her to insist that her partner wear a condom *every* time she has sexual relations, no matter what type of contraception *she* might be using. Aside from the pregnancy issue, her partner's wearing a condom is also necessary to help prevent the spread of any sexually transmitted diseases either partner might be carrying.

DATE RAPE

Eighteen-year-old Sandy has not seemed herself in the past few months. Normally active and vivacious, she's dropped many of her interests, and her grades are going down. When you confront her about these changes, she tears up and confesses that she has been troubled since the past summer when she was a victim of date rape.

As is true after any rape, a girl may ask herself, *What did I do to cause this to happen to me?* In a date rape, the sense of "having asked for it" can be even stronger, since the girl had consented to going out on a date with the offender. Filled with a sense of guilt and shame, the victim often doesn't tell anyone about the event, which keeps her from working through the emotional issues that are involved.

Let your daughter know that you are glad she's opened up about this matter, as doing so represents the start of her healing. Encourage her to tell you what happened in her particular case, exploring all the feelings she experienced. Typically, she'll feel angry and betrayed in addition to the guilt and shame she's been carrying. The fact that date rape is particularly hard to prove adds to the victim's sense of impotence and frustration. Reassure your daughter that no matter how she might have behaved, her date still did not have the right to force her to have sex once she said no.

But what if you feel that your daughter used very poor judgment, making the possibility of a date rape more likely (e.g., by meeting a boy in a club and, knowing nothing about him, accepting an invitation to leave the club and go somewhere else with him; by letting a boy drive her to a remote area without knowing him well; by making out with a boy early in a relationship and conveying the attitude that she takes sex lightly)? How can you let her know that she made an error without sounding accusatory, as if you are blaming her for what happened?

A good method is to ask if, in hindsight, she feels that there was any way she might have anticipated such a problem. Chances are she'll mention the point you're wanting her to make. If not, you can tell her that you think it's very difficult to anticipate a boy's character without knowing a lot about him; consequently, the best way to be safe is to use caution in putting herself in any situation where she is alone with a boy she doesn't know well. Also, remind her that alcohol or drug involvement (hers or the boy's) compromises her safety even more. Then tell her directly that no matter what mistakes she might have made due to inexperience, the male is still at fault if he performs any sexual activity with her without her permission.

If your teen's emotional state doesn't seem to improve once she's confessed her secret, suggest that she consult a mental health professional. There may be details that she could not feel comfortable telling a parent, and a therapist can help her sort out her feelings.

In addition to helping your teen deal with the emotional aspects of date rape, you may also wonder whether or not to press charges against the offender. Many parents want to pursue legal recourse; teens rarely agree. Date rape is very difficult to prove, and a girl must be prepared to have her character and any past sexual history carefully scrutinized if she presses charges. Certainly, consultation with an attorney and/or a mental health professional would be appropriate to determine the wisdom of legal action in your specific situation.

SLEEPING TOGETHER

Nineteen-year-old Rob is coming home for spring break and is bringing with him the girlfriend he's met in college. After they arrive, he pulls you aside and tells you that the two of them have been sleeping together for some time. Naturally, they want to stay in the same room during their vacation at your house.

Your reaction to this situation will obviously depend on your own view about such matters. You might decide to allow your son and his girlfriend to sleep together, since they're doing so anyway. If you're very opposed to premarital sex, you'll insist that they sleep in separate rooms. The point is it is *your* home, and you have the right to ask others to respect your own value system within its walls. Realize, however, that if you say no to their sleeping together, your son might visit you less often until he's married!

E I G H T

ALCOHOL/DRUGS

T he fact is that it is *illegal* in every state for a person to drink alcohol until that person has reached a certain minimum age, usually twenty-one. Other nonprescription drugs are illegal at any age. Unfortunately, most teenagers do some experimenting with alcohol/drugs in spite of the legalities.

Parents differ widely in response to such experimentation. Some believe that it is naive to think that most teens today won't drink alcohol sometime during their adolescence and that a parent's job is to teach a teen how to use moderation, discretion, and safety if and when he does drink. Other parents think that a teen's drinking is absolutely inappropriate, except perhaps for religious purposes or for special-occasion family dinners.

If you adhere to the first philosophy, you'll educate your adolescent about not driving a car after drinking, about designated drivers, and about eating food when drinking to reduce the rate of potential intoxication. You'll give him your ideas about what you consider an appropriate, or moderate, quantity to drink. You'll tell him that if he ever has too much to drink to drive home (or if the driver giving him a ride has been drinking, and your teen does not have a driver's license), he is to telephone you and you will gladly come get him (and any other passengers) and transport everyone to safety, with no penalty to him. You might also serve alcohol to his friends under your supervision, making sure that nobody gets drunk or, if they do, that they spend the night at your house.

If you take the second approach, you will give your teenager a clear message that he is not to drink. Period. If he does, you'll enforce immediate consequences. Parents in the first group will only begin to set consequences if they feel that their adolescent is beginning to *abuse* alcohol. Of course, both groups of parents typically think that the parents in the other group are dead wrong!

When it comes to the other drugs, most parents do not want their teens even to experiment. However, the parents in the first group might be more liberal, becoming concerned only if they think their adolescent could be crossing the line between "experimentation" and "abuse."

Whichever group you identify with, you will certainly want to give your teenager some basic information about the legal issues surrounding alcohol/drug use. Make it clear that, for him, any alcohol/drug use is illegal, and explain the trouble he can get into with the law should he get caught (you'll need to check the specific penalties in your state of residence for "Minor in Possession of Alcohol" and for "Driving While Intoxicated"—DWI—charges). Penalties can include fines, probation, community service, time in jail, and/or loss of a driver's license. Also, be sure to explain the liability involved if someone gets hurt or killed, either as a result of your teen's alcohol/drug use or as a result of that person's being given alcohol/drugs in your home.

You'll also want to caution him about alcohol poisoning. This situation occurs when a person has consumed more alcohol than the body can process (more likely in younger people) and results in a stuporous state in which the victim cannot be roused. Unfortunately, a person can be obviously drunk but seem to be fine; when he goes to sleep, however, he may move into a toxic, stuporous state that can result in permanent disability or death if he does not receive immediate treatment. Consequently, your teen should know that a drunk friend who passes out should be roused and forced to stay awake (walking the victim around the room can be helpful) until the alcohol has metabolized out of his system (rather than "letting him sleep it off"). If the person cannot be awakened, or becomes more groggy after being awakened, Emergency Medical Services—EMS—should be called.

Ideally, you will have begun to educate your teen about alcohol/drug issues *before* he is an adolescent. Now that he's a teenager, however, you can go into more detail about alcohol/drug addiction, how it gets started, and how to recognize when experimentation stops and dependence begins.

Because teen alcohol/drug abuse is a complicated problem, there are entire books written on this subject alone. This chapter is intended only to give a brief overview of some important points for you to consider when raising your teenager. By the way, I am using the term *alcohol/drugs* to emphasize the point that alcohol *is* a drug, just like cocaine, marijuana, uppers, downers, or any other mood-altering substance. Although our culture and lawmakers treat alcohol differently than the other drugs, the symptoms of misuse and dependence remain basically the same for both.

WHY TEENS USE ALCOHOL/DRUGS

Teenagers may use alcohol/drugs because of curiosity, excitement, peer pressure, and/or rebellion. They may turn to these substances to boost a sagging self-esteem, to feel more grown-up, or to escape unpleasant or painful feelings, such as anxiety, frustration, anger, or depression.

Today's teens also face tremendous external pressures that contribute to alcohol/drug use. They live in an instant-gratification culture, typically expecting things to happen "now," without necessarily having to work for them. Alcohol/drugs work rapidly to produce a feeling change and require no effort to do it. Also, adolescents are encouraged both by their peers and by society to use chemicals; our billboards and magazines bombard them with messages that drinking something alcoholic will make them attractive, sexy, and successful. And, in spite of the law, the fact is that alcohol/drugs are readily available in most communities.

DIFFERENCES BETWEEN ADULT AND TEEN ALCOHOL/ DRUG USE

Adults and teens differ in the way they use alcohol/drugs. Adults tend to prefer one or two mood-altering chemicals; teens are more likely to use anything that's available. Adults who don't have an alcohol/drug problem will seldom plan to get drunk or high; teens see getting drunk or high as their *goal* when they are ready to "party."

With teens, it's much harder to distinguish between "abuse" and "addiction"; what would be considered symptoms of chemical dependence in adults are often just typical behaviors for adolescents who drink alcohol. For example, one sign of late-stage chemical dependence in adults is morning drinking (usually to stave off "withdrawal" symptoms, such as the shakes and nausea). But teens who use alcohol/drugs often do so in the morning, going to school stoned or drunk just because it's the "thing to do." They may be chemically dependent, but not always; they may be crying out for attention and help, or they may have other motives.

Also, hiding alcohol/drug use from friends, family, and co-workers is considered a symptom of chemical dependence in adults. For teens, however, hiding the use of such substances is almost required in order to keep the adolescent out of trouble with parents, teachers, or the police. The act of hiding the behavior, per se, would not be a reliable indicator of chemical dependence in a teen.

Also, addiction occurs faster in teens than in adults. It can take many years for a thirty-year-old to reach the chronic stages of alcoholism; the teen under fifteen who is abusing the same amount of alcohol can reach the same stage in less than fifteen months.

Most important, adults who begin to abuse alcohol/drugs have the advantage of having completed most of the tasks of their adolescent emotional development and have mastered some life skills. When they stop abusing, they have this prior emotional development to fall back on. But teens who abuse alcohol/drugs are *developmentally arrested* at the point at which they began to abuse; when they *stop* using these substances, many remain emotionally fixated at the age they began heavy usage. They've never learned to deal with their feelings in a mature way and have missed out on learning important social, academic, and/or vocational skills. If they quit abusing these substances, whether at eighteen or at twenty-five, all of the developmental tasks of adolescence are still ahead of them.

FROM EXPERIMENTATION TO ADDICTION

There are a number of ways that experts in the substance-abuse field categorize the "stages" a person goes through in becoming dependent on or addicted to alcohol/drugs. All essentially describe the process whereby a person increasingly loses *choice* and *control* over his usage. A system I like for its practicality and applicability to teenagers is the one described by Dick Schaefer of the Johnson Institute (an alcohol/drug treatment center in Minneapolis, Minnesota). A summary of this view follows:

PHASE I. LEARNS MOOD SWING (USE)

When a teen is first introduced to alcohol or another drug, he quickly discovers that it can produce a mood swing, which is usually experienced as positive and fun. He learns that he can trust this substance to work quickly and reliably, every time. He also learns that he can control the degree of the mood alteration by varying the amount of the substance: one beer makes him feel good, two or three make him feel even better. Important, when his buzz or high wears off, he returns to a normal feeling state and his normal lifestyle.

PHASE II. SEEKS MOOD SWING (MISUSE)

The teen begins to apply what he's learned in Phase I to social situations and typically starts making a few self-imposed rules about using the drug ("I'll only drink at weekend parties"; "I'll only have one six-pack"). At this stage, the teen begins to experience a few of the milder consequences of using alcohol/drugs, such as hangovers or a fuzzy-headed feeling, but *returns* to normal feelings and behaviors after the high wears off. Most so-called social drinkers and recreational drug users are in this phase.

PHASE III. HARMFUL DEPENDENCE (ABUSE)

This is the phase where a teen begins to be chemically dependent. Why some teens progress to this stage and others don't is still not clear, but what *happens* is predictable. The teen begins to experience physical, emotional, social, academic, vocational, and/or spiritual losses. His behavior shows a more intense preoccupation with alcohol/drugs, an increasing tolerance to it, and the repeated breaking of his self-imposed rules. He begins to develop a delusional system made of up several psychological defenses: denial ("I don't have a drinking problem"), rationalization ("I just drank too much because it was a bad day at school"), minimizing ("I only had *four* beers!"), and projection ("*You're* the one with the problem. If you'd leave me alone, I'd be just fine!").

In this stage, teens often begin to experience memory loss while drinking (blackouts); when they are sober, they don't remember specific things they did or said during the drinking episode. Blackouts should not be confused with a loss of consciousness (passing out). Teens may also experience a different type of memory distortion, called euphoric states, where they remember isolated incidents during their prior drinking bout with an *exaggerated* sense of how great it felt to be high.

The memory distortion from blackouts and euphoric states, plus the psychological defenses listed above, combine to prevent a teen from consciously experiencing painful feelings of remorse, guilt, shame, anger, anxiety, hurt, self-hate, and even despair.

PHASE IV. DRINKS/USES TO FEEL NORMAL (ADDICTION)

At this point, the teen experiences deterioration in all phases of his life. Thoughts of suicide may begin, and suicide attempts may be made. He begins to use his favorite substance(s) to get back to feeling "normal." In this late addiction stage, an intervention must be made, or the teen will die.

In the vignettes later in this chapter, I'll describe specific situations that represent the four phases of alcohol/drug use, giving appropriate interventions and consequences for each.

WHAT CAUSES ADDICTION?

Most experts in the substance-abuse field consider chemical dependence, or addiction, to be a disease. A person has this disease if the chemical of choice becomes more important than anything else in that person's life. But addiction is not caused by a character flaw, low self-control, irresponsibility, or some other personal shortcoming. No one is to blame for another person's chemical dependence, so parents of addicted teenagers do not need to feel guilty that they've "done something wrong" as parents.

There seems to be a genetic predisposition to alcoholism in some people, especially when their biological parents or grandparents are alcoholics. When genetics plays a role, the chemical dependence generally develops in the teen years, and early drinking experiences are remembered later to have been excessive in nature.

In addition to the genetic alcoholic, there is the stress-induced alcoholic. These people generally develop chemical dependency in midlife or late-life when career, home, kids, and marriage create high stress. They have often been able to drink socially without significant consequences during their young-adult years.

Another type of chemically dependent person is called the habituated alcoholic. This person typically will not develop the addiction until later in life. He's likely to be someone who has developed a habit of frequent drinking (with clients, for example), and he becomes *physically* addicted to alcohol.

Those who hold alcohol/drug addiction to be a disease feel that it *causes* the person to develop physical or emotional disorders, rather than that such disorders cause the alcohol/drug abuse. This means that the other problems a chemically dependent person has, such as physical illness, depression, unresolved grief, trouble at school or on the job, or disturbed family relationships, cannot be treated effectively until the person *stops* using chemicals.

This disease model of substance abuse presupposes that, once addicted, the chemically dependent person can never safely use the substance again. Consequently, the victim must accept the need for continued abstinence the rest of his life; most adult alcoholics who begin drinking again, even after years of sobriety, will quickly, if not immediately, return to their former level of addiction.

Some take issue with this hard-line "once an addict, always an addict" position, especially with teenagers. Because there is so much peer pressure to drink at this stage in one's life (and extending into the college years), many question the wisdom of telling a teenager who has reached the stage of addiction that he can *never* use alcohol/drugs again without progressing into a fatal condition if untreated. Certainly, there are adolescents who seek treatment for alcohol addiction and then return to a stage of drinking where they once again show choice and control. The question becomes, Will they again return to addiction later in their lives? Or, perhaps, should our definition of *addiction* in teens be reevaluated? Moreover, there are reports of adults who by all definitions would be considered addicted to alcohol but who, after not using it for years, begin to drink socially without progressing into an addicted state. It is to be hoped that further research will be able to clarify these issues.

ENABLING

Enabling is a term used to describe any behavior that keeps another person from getting real help, resulting in it being easier for an alcohol/drug user to *continue* to use such substances. Enablers, then, are people who take responsibility for the behavior, feelings, and decisions of the user and who try to control or rescue him. With teens, enablers are usually parents and other family members, but they can also be teachers, coaches, clergymen, and other authority figures (even some mental health professionals). Enablers mean well and usually act out of love, concern, and/or fear for the user. However, the end result of their behavior is to keep the user from experiencing the consequences of his alcohol/drug use and from getting appropriate help.

An enabler's behavior may be caretaking ("Let me help you clean up the vomit and get you some clean sheets"), accusing ("You know we don't allow you to smoke pot, and here you are, *stoned*!"), threatening ("If you ever do this again, we're selling your car"), laying blame elsewhere ("I knew those friends of yours were a rotten influence!"), guilt-inducing ("How could you do this to us after all we've done for you?"), excusing ("Well, boys will be boys!"), assuming responsibility ("I know that my going back to work has been stressful for you"), laying down the law ("There will be no more using cocaine, and that's that!"), expressing helplessness ("I knew I could never raise a teenager!"), or provoking ("What's the matter with you? Don't you have a brain left in your head?").

In all of these examples, the parent has taken the teen off the hook and helped him to avoid any actual consequences of his behavior. Instead, the parent has taken the consequences upon himself and *enabled* the teen to continue using alcohol/drugs.

Other examples of enabling behaviors include

- Being afraid to confront your teen when you discover evidence of his substance use, such as beer cans in his trash basket or a roach clip in his sock drawer
- Snooping in your teen's room or listening in on his phone calls because you don't trust him
- Feeling guilty and inadequate as a parent because your teen is using
- Denying that your teen really has a problem because he is still making passing grades in school, kisses you good night, usually comes home by his curfew, and so on
- Feeling hurt and unappreciated by your teen
- Focusing on the pressures your teen is experiencing
- Becoming a dictator in an attempt to gain control
- Blaming your teen's friends for his using
- Excusing your teen from doing chores, participating in family outings, getting to school on time, and so on

- Thinking that your teen will "grow out of it"
- Telling yourself that it's normal for teens to get drunk/stoned
- Beginning to doubt your own perceptions, thinking that you must be overreacting
- Avoiding seeking help for yourself and/or your teen because you fear the stigma of doing so
- Becoming overprotective of your teen in an effort to minimize your teen's chances of using
- Feeling angry with your spouse because of your teen's behavior
- Blaming yourself for not being a better parent
- Bailing your teen out when he's in trouble, such as paying his fines, doing his homework, or covering his bounced checks
- Keeping your teen's alcohol/drug use a secret from other family members
- Allowing your teen to use alcohol/drugs for other than religious occasions or traditional family celebrations
- Using illicit drugs (either parent)
- Serving alcohol to your teen's friends
- Getting drunk in front of your teen

To stop enabling your teen to use alcohol/drugs, you will need to do two things. First, you must give him the consistent message that *he* is responsible for his own feelings, behaviors, and decisions. Second, you must allow him to experience the *consequences* of his alcohol/drug use. By doing these two things, you'll be becoming responsible *to* your teen rather than trying to be responsible *for* him.

SIGNS THAT YOUR TEEN MAY BE ABUSING ALCOHOL/DRUGS

Harry Croft, M.D., psychiatrist, has coined a simple way to think about signs of alcohol/drug abuse in teens, called the Five P's:

- A change in **Personality**
- A change in **Peer** group
- A change in **Performance** (at home or at school)
- **Physical** signs and symptoms

- **Paraphernalia** (spoons, mirrors, straightedge razor blades, bongs, roach clips, roach-clip earrings, etc.)

To illustrate, let's look at a vignette of a typical teenager who is abusing alcohol/drugs. Certainly, your teen might not exhibit all of these signs, but they are included so that you can consider them as possible "red flags."

Basically, your teen seems to be "a different person" since she entered junior high school, showing significant personality changes. It is getting harder for her to get up in the morning on time, and she may be sleeping most of the day and staying up most of the night. She's changed friends, and now hangs out with a group of teens who are considered "troublemakers" or a "bad influence" by teachers and other parents.

She treats her home as if it were a motel, avoiding family members and escaping into her music. She constantly seems to be testing the house rules, especially about curfews and chores. She seems to be getting increasingly oppositional, and is beginning to be hostile and mistrustful of authority figures.

She's increased her fluid intake, especially sodas with caffeine, milk, and/or water, and snacks almost continually on carbohydrates (she's got the "munchies"). She's using over-the-counter eyedrops (to reduce redness) and breath mints or gum (to cover the odor of alcohol). She's having problems maintaining grades that are commensurate with her abilities and is getting into trouble for her behavior at school (perhaps being expelled). She's dishonest, has a decreased attention span, and seems more "sensitive" or irritable than average. She's seemed to have lost interest in activities and pastimes that she used to like, and is preoccupied with privacy and secrecy.

She may have been fired from a job, and she may have stolen from a family member or others (or has been accused of doing so). You (or the police) have caught her in possession of alcohol/drugs at least once; in return, she's become defensive and tried to turn the situation around by blaming you ("You never trust me!"). She may be experimenting with a number of drugs, has increased the frequency of her use, and may be using them in inappropriate settings (at school or at work). She may begin to buy her drugs from people she doesn't know, and exhibits "junkie talk" about getting high. She may seem increasingly paranoid and insecure, and she hangs around with peers who have low self-regard.

Again, your teen might not exhibit all, or even most, of the disturbing behaviors in the above scenario. They are included as an aid in helping you to recognize a possible "red flag" if you notice its appearance in your adolescent.

COMMON DILEMMAS

Although there are parents who would take issue with the stance of forbidding a teen to use alcohol/drugs other than for religious or special family occasions, I'm going to use this more conservative approach in the situations that follow. The reason for this is that many parents who allow their teens to use alcohol (and even other drugs) do so *not* because they really believe that's the best stance but because they feel helpless to do otherwise. The system described in the incidents below illustrates a way that parents *can* enforce the legal position involving alcohol/drugs if they so choose.

"BUT *YOU* DO IT!"

Thirteen-year-old Tom is removing the trash after you've had a few friends over for the evening. Seeing all the beer cans and wine cooler bottles, he asks why you drink when you won't allow him to do so.

You don't need to be defensive about this question; just let your teen know that being an adult gives a person certain privileges. Drinking alcohol, driving a car, and getting a loan from the bank are examples of actions that legally require a person to be a certain minimum age.

Of course, if you or your mate are getting drunk in front of your adolescent, his question could represent an indirect way of complaining about your behavior. It could be very difficult for him to confront you about having a drinking problem. So ask him how he feels about your drinking, if he notices any changes in your behavior when you do, and if he's ever felt embarrassed about it. Then listen carefully.

A similar question might occur if you or your mate use illegal drugs and your teen discovers it. If this is the case, you have the choice of admitting that you're addicted, if true, or of explaining your philosophy about using that particular substance. Either way, it would be wise to seriously consider giving up your drug use, and pledging this to your teen. After all, if you continue using and "hope you don't get caught," you're only encouraging law breaking and risk taking. Realize, too, that drug-using parents have been turned in to the police by angry teenagers.

Remember that no matter how you justify your own alcohol/ drug use, your behavior has a powerful modeling effect on your adolescent. No matter what your words, your actions will speak louder.

THE WISH TO EXPERIMENT

Fifteen-year-old Martin takes issue with your policy of no drug use. He wants to know, "What's wrong with trying a drug just once to see what it's like? Otherwise, I'll never know!"

Some parents try to answer this question by elaborating about all the awful things that have happened to people who get hooked on drugs. Besides not answering the question, rest assured that your teen knows (or will know) many teens who experiment with a drug once or several times, who don't become addicted, and who don't have anything terrible happen as a consequence.

What you can tell your teen is that, first of all, using drugs is *breaking the law*. Second, a person has no way of knowing whether he or she is a *potential addict*. One might *intend* to use a drug only once to see its effects and then find that he or she just can't resist doing it again. After all, if you do something once and you suffer no ill effects, it's all the more tempting to do it again if the opportunity presents itself. It's *after* using a drug "experimentally" that one can gradually become addicted.

As for the "How will I ever know what it's like?" question, remind your teen that there are many illegal and/or dangerous activities that one might find exciting but that, hopefully, he will not choose to do! This might include everything from robbing a bank to diving into a body of water without knowing its depth.

SUSPECTING ALCOHOL/DRUG USE

Fifteen-year-old Josh has become very irritable lately. His grades are dropping, he seems like a different person, and he's hanging around with kids you suspect are a negative influence. Although you haven't caught him with drugs or found any drug paraphernalia, you think he might be using them, in spite of his denials when you have confronted him.

Wait until a time when you *strongly* suspect that your teen has very recently used drugs (for example, after he's sneaked out at night or when he's behaving strangely in the morning after being with friends the night before). Then, without warning him in advance, pick up your teen from school and tell him you've arranged for him to see his physician for a physical. Let him know that you are concerned about his irritability, dropping grades, and whatever else is problematic, and that the first step in evaluating what might be wrong is to get him a physical checkup. The doctor has agreed to see him that afternoon. What you don't tell him is that you've called the doctor prior to the visit and have asked him to do a drug screen along with the regular blood work and urinalysis that are part of a physical examination. Your teen never needs to know that a drug screen was done, unless it's positive.

If the blood work shows that your teen has been using drugs, you will need to confront him with this information. He will no doubt be very angry that you tricked him; your explanation is that you genuinely had reason to suspect drug use, that you didn't want to accuse him falsely, but that, in fact, you were right. Let him know that in situations of such importance to his well-being, you felt you needed to take this step. Then let him know that the important issue now really is not about how you found out about his drug use; what matters is that the problem is out in the open, and you can now get professional help to determine the next appropriate step.

If the drug screen is negative, your doctor might find some other physical condition that would help explain your son's behavior. If nothing physically wrong is found, consult a mental health professional for evaluation of the underlying problem.

When an adolescent's drug use is suspected, many parents feel justified in violating their teen's personal privacy. They eavesdrop or tape their teen's phone conversations, search his room and closet, read his diaries or journals, and look through his backpack (or her purse). However, such behavior sets up a breach of trust in the teen who finds out about it. These measures should be taken by parents only if they have *strong* reason to suspect that a teen is thinking of or planning to commit suicide or homicide, or if their teen's physical or emotional health is in *serious* jeopardy. Some professionals also recommend that a thorough room or closet clean-out by a parent is appropriate if a teen is in an inpatient treatment setting for chemical dependence, but that the teen be told in advance that this will be done.

FINDING EVIDENCE OF ALCOHOL/DRUG USE

Sixteen-year-old Randy is having a late football practice, so you decide to do him a favor by putting his laundry away. In the process, you discover a bag of marijuana in his drawer.

Whether or not your teen admits that the drug is his (he'll probably tell you that he's keeping it for a friend), let him know that his possession or use is illegal. Then set up a "No Use Contract"*: no drinking if he is underage, no possession or use of other drugs,

---

*While most mental health and substance abuse professionals recommend a contract system, the specific contract names and details I'm using are the system described by Dick Schaefer in his book *Choices and Consequences* (see "Suggested Reading").

and no illegal actions related to alcohol/drug use (such as containers of alcohol that have been opened or drug paraphernalia in the car). In order for this contract to be effective, you'll need to let your teen know *in advance* what the consequences will be should he violate it. Tell him that you will follow through with whatever guidelines have been established by his school and/or by the community for alcohol/drug use.

For example, in most schools, teens who are caught possessing alcohol or drugs are not allowed to participate in school activities for a specified period of time. Consequently, if your adolescent violated the No Use Contract, you would notify the school officials, and he would have to accept the penalty. Or, if your teen were picked up and arrested by the police for using alcohol/drugs, you would let him spend the night in jail rather than rushing down in the middle of the night to rescue him from the natural consequences of his actions.

This plan might sound harsh to you, and it might make your teen very angry with you. You might even be criticized harshly by your relatives, the football coach, or whomever. But remember, you are doing much more than enforcing the consequences set up by the school and the court: You are letting your teen know in no uncertain terms that *he* is responsible for his choices and that you will not rescue him from the consequences.

You might also want to add your own time-limited consequences in addition to stipulating those regarding the school and the court. These could include loss of phone or driving privileges, an earlier curfew, or attendance at a program about chemical dependence. You can show respect for your adolescent by building choice into his consequences whenever possible ("You may attend the community program next week about substance abuse, or you may give up your telephone privileges for two weeks").

Notice that you *do not* need to interpret your teen's behavior by labeling him an "abuser" or an "addict." And you don't have to yell, threaten, lecture, or accuse. Remember that it's up to your teen to show that he *isn't* chemically dependent by abiding by the terms of the agreement you've worked out together. That is his responsibility; yours is to control his environment by setting appropriate limits.

COMING HOME DRUNK

Fourteen-year-old Amanda comes home from a school dance obviously intoxicated. She immediately begins throwing up and continues to do so throughout the night.

Of course, the first thing you would want to do is to establish that your teen is physically safe. You'd want to determine how much alcohol she's had, whether she's taken any other drugs, and if there's a possibility of an overdose or alcohol poisoning (see page 145). If you're not sure, you could call a poison control center to determine whether or not you need to get her to the emergency room of your local hospital.

Once you've determined that she's okay from a physical standpoint, you would probably choose to take care of her *if this is the first time* she's come home in this condition. If not, *don't* take care of her (other than making sure that she's not in physical danger and is not behaving dangerously). This means *not* holding her head over the toilet, *not* bringing her cold cloths, and *not* cleaning up after her. Let her sleep wherever she falls asleep, checking periodically to see that she is not in a position to swallow and choke on her vomit and that she can be roused. Do not attempt to confront her about her behavior while she's still under the influence of any drug; let her know you'll talk with her in the morning.

The next day, talk with your teen about her behavior of the night before. Don't try to have this conversation if you are angry; wait until you feel calm and in control. At this point, you would set up your No Use Contract, if you haven't done so already, and set whatever consequences you think are appropriate.

If this is a second offense and she has violated the No Use Contract, repeat the consequences you've already specified and put them into effect. For example, you might tell her that she will be grounded from all activities for two weeks, but that she can reduce the penalty to one week if she attends a program about chemical dependence. Ask her what her choice will be and then monitor her behavior to make sure she follows through with it.

If your adolescent shows you that she can follow the No Use Contract, and she does not have another incident of using alcohol/drugs, you know that she is still in control of such behavior. If not, you would move on to the next level of confrontation (see the "Simple Contract," next situation).

A LEGAL CHARGE

The telephone rings at two A.M. It's seventeen-year-old Dale calling from jail. He's been charged with Minor in Possession of Alcohol.

While your parental instinct might be to rush down to the jail (or to a detention center) to pick up your son, resist it. Having to spend the night in a "drunk tank" (or a center) is a consequence that is likely to make an impact. Ask him to tell you what happened and then tell him you'll pick him up in the morning. Ideally, you would have told him in advance that this would be your reaction should such a situation ever occur.

It's likely that a teen who has been charged with Minor in Possession is at least at the "misuse" stage, that is, he is using alcohol/drugs regularly. Teens at this level typically have broken the law by using at a party, in school, or in a car. Schoolwork has usually been affected. Consequences for breaking the law might be jail time and/or probation. If the school is involved, participation in school-sponsored activities and/or suspension may occur.

If your teen has had any of these consequences, or has broken the No Use Contract, it's time to implement a Simple Contract. This is a *written* agreement between you and your teenager with non-negotiable rules that include no chemical use, no violence, and attendance at a group on chemical dependence (sometimes held at schools, via the court, or at agencies/hospitals in the community). You would also impose some restriction of your teen's privileges at home for a limited time (limited or no use of the car or phone, grounding from weekend activities, etc.). The contract would expire in a specified number of weeks, or until the intervention group or class is completed.

If any rules of the Simple Contract are broken, consequences (also written into the contract) would include an evaluation by a chemical dependence counselor or other mental health professional, attendance at a more involved (several meetings) meeting or class on chemical dependence, and a "Turf Contract" (see next situation). If he's able to follow the Simple Contract without violating *any* rule, he's letting you know that he is still able to exercise choice about using or not using alcohol/drugs.

Obviously, your monitoring of the contract will be essential. This does not mean that you should interrogate your teen or search his room, listen in on his phone conversations, read his journal, or otherwise invade his privacy. Express your concerns calmly, and make time to connect emotionally with your teen. Take advantage of spontaneous moments for conversation with him, and plan time regularly (a couple of hours) to do something you both enjoy. If you are having significant family problems, or if your teen lets you know that he's having some personal problem, consult a mental health professional.

WHEN YOUR TEEN KEEPS ON USING

Fifteen-year-old Kendall is caught at school with LSD in her purse. This isn't the first time she has been caught using an illegal substance, and she has already attended a group for education about chemical dependence. You've already implemented the No Use Contract, as well as the Simple Contract.

This is a Phase III, or "abuse," situation. Your teen is likely to be preoccupied with alcohol/drugs, she's probably doing poorly in school, she's likely to have broken several home rules, and she may have primarily alcohol/drug–using friends. At this level, she's liable to be very defensive about her use when she's confronted about it. She's likely to be furious with you when you try to talk with her about the school incident, may blame both you and/or the school for being out to get her, and may rationalize that "everybody else is doing it, they just didn't get caught." This is the time to implement the Turf Contract.

This more restrictive *written* contract includes all the nonnegotiable rules of the Simple Contract. It also includes *specific behaviors* that will be required in order for her to have certain home privileges (a late curfew, use of the phone, etc.) or school privileges (participation in sports or other activities). Points are assigned to each behavior, and the granting of privileges depends on the teen's earning 90 percent of the *possible* total points. Privileges depend on her following the *total contract*, rather than on any one behavior. *No exceptions or special occasions are allowed.* This contract would also include a renegotiation date when all privileges and consequences are reviewed, rather than a specific end point (as in the Simple Contract).

Some chemical dependence professionals also recommend that by the time a teen has reached the Phase III stage, a provision for *unscheduled* drug screens be written into any contract. This means that the teen must agree to have a drug screen whenever a parent requests it. Also, such a provision is often recommended when a teen returns home from an inpatient treatment program for substance abuse; many adolescents are vulnerable to returning to alcohol/drug use when they are no longer under the tight control and monitoring they experienced in the hospital. They are less likely to relapse if they know they must remain accountable.

Your teen might insist that the Turf Contract is totally ridiculous because she is only "experimenting" and is not addicted to any drug. Let her know that indeed she might not be addicted, and you hope that she isn't. However, it isn't your job to prove that she is; it's *her* job to show you that she *isn't* by following this contract. If she can't follow it, this will demonstrate that she's out of control and needs more help.

Consequences for breaking this contract would include treatment for chemical dependence: Your teen would be given a choice between treatment in an outpatient and treatment in an inpatient setting. She would also be required to go to individual counseling/therapy and would be put on the "Bottom-Line Contract."

By the time a teenager needs a Turf Contract, she may be quite oppositional or hostile to you. Tension and power struggles may seem like the norm at home. It can be very helpful at this point to seek counseling for yourself and your mate (if you haven't already) regarding the problems at home. It's also wise to become involved in a support group for parents of teens who abuse alcohol/drugs. Being able to open up about your adolescent's substance-abuse problems with other parents who are going through the same kinds of things can lessen your sense of isolation and can give you emotional comfort and support.

If an adolescent cannot follow the Turf Contract, she's lost control and choice regarding her alcohol/drug use. Symptoms at this point are considered to be progressive and chronic. Teens have died, or have caused others to die, as a result. Many become increasingly depressed and may attempt, or commit, suicide.

The Bottom-Line Contract, like the Turf Contract, is based on a point system and outlines in writing the specific things a teen must do in order to continue living at home and staying in school. All privileges are suspended for two weeks while the teen demonstrates that she can get a minimum of 90 percent of her total points each week. If she's unable to meet these specifications, she has the choice, if at all possible, of entering one of two *inpatient* treatment settings. There is no choice about whether or not she enters treatment; her choice is only about *where* she'll have treatment.

If your teen is unable to go to an inpatient treatment setting (if your insurance won't allow it and you cannot afford it; or if she does not qualify for a state program), you'll need to check with your local chemical dependency treatment centers to find out what options are available within your community for chemically dependent adolescents.

WHEN YOU NO LONGER HAVE CONTROL

Eighteen-year-old Mike has dropped out of school and has continued to abuse alcohol/drugs in spite of your getting treatment for him. He refuses to abide by any contract, and you've discovered that he's bringing drugs into your home.

You're not doing your son any favor by allowing him to remain at home at this point. Furthermore, you're allowing your teen to set a poor example for any other children who remain at home. At his age, you have no control over him legally or otherwise; you cannot make him enter treatment (he has to agree to it voluntarily). By allowing the status quo to continue, you are enabling him to continue his self-destructive behavior.

You might wonder if you could arrange to have your son involuntarily committed to a treatment program. This is very difficult in most states and usually requires that a person be of *imminent* danger either to himself or to others. Even if a person has stated that he is going to kill himself or someone else, if he can lucidly convince a psychiatrist or judge that he has changed his mind or did not mean what he said, he usually cannot be committed.

Difficult as this may be, you'll need to ask your son to leave home. If you decide to pay for something for him, make your check out to the person whom you intend to receive the money (the landlord, a physician, etc.) and mail it directly to the appropriate person. Rather than giving him money for groceries, it would be best to buy the items yourself and give them to him. These precautions will ensure that your money will not be used to buy alcohol/drugs.

You may be terrified that your adolescent will get into even more trouble if you force him to leave home. You worry that he might not get or keep a job and that he could resort to writing hot checks, stealing, or doing something else that would result in his getting arrested. You fear that he might move in with other drug users, or even drug dealers, or that he will "hit bottom" and become suicidal.

All of these fears are understandable and, unfortunately, *could* happen. However, your teen might also use this opportunity of being forced to go on his own to get himself on a more productive path. Even if your worst fears are confirmed, your adolescent may be a person who will not turn things around for himself *unless* he hits bottom. Consequently, your taking this important action may be the very thing that saves him. What *is* certain is that your supporting his chemically dependent behavior by allowing him to remain at home will do nothing to help him change his self-destructive behavior.

If you require your teen to leave home, chances are high that he'll be very angry with you. He'll accuse you of trying to get rid of him, of not caring, of not loving him, and of "kicking" him out. He may threaten not to see you again and might, in fact, stay away from you for long periods of time.

Many teens who are out of control drive a wedge between their parents, increasing the household tension before they leave home. Often, parents begin to blame each other for their adolescent's problematic behavior. Because they can't agree on what to do, they become even more inconsistent with their teen and undermine each other even more. Conflicts begin to escalate, and the marital relationship may begin to fall apart. Also, if something bad does occur after a teen leaves home, the parent who did not want the adolescent to leave will typically blame the other parent for what occurred.

If you see this beginning to happen within your marriage, it is highly recommended that you find a support group of parents in similar circumstances, such as Tough Love (or start one if none is available). Such a group can be of great help when you are preparing to ask your teenager to leave home, as well as during and after the time that he actually leaves. If his behavior doesn't change, if he gets into trouble and wants to come home, a support group will see you through the really tough decisions ahead.

Every parent wants to be a good parent. It's very difficult when you are in the throes of this type of family conflict to see that insisting that your adolescent leave home *is* being a good parent. Moreover, seldom do *both* parents agree at the same time (or ever) that this course of action is the one to be taken. If anything happens to the teen, a marriage can quickly become seriously jeopardized if the couple doesn't get professional help.

On a more positive note, for many teens who are out of control and are made to leave home and take responsibility for themselves, it is this strong action by the parents that saves them from a destructive life course. The courageous action of parents forces the older teen to begin assuming total responsibility for his choices. Sometimes it is the hard life lessons that enable young adults to create their own triumphs.

NINE

"RED FLAGS" FOR POTENTIALLY SERIOUS PROBLEMS

With the storms of adolescence, most parents expect that they might have to face a few problem situations with their teenager. Sometimes, however, there's a question about how serious the problem might be.

It could be a single statement that sets off the alarm (e.g., a teen says she's thinking of killing herself). Or it might be that some problematic behavior gradually emerges into a pattern, warranting greater concern (e.g., his bad temper turns into increasing explosiveness, culminating in his putting his hand through his bedroom window).

Distinguishing a normal adolescent problem from a more serious one can be a fine line to draw. In this chapter, I'll give some guidelines for you to consider in making such a distinction, pointing out some common red-flag situations whose importance should not be minimized.

RECOGNIZING A RED FLAG

Before we look at some specific problem areas that can signal serious trouble for teens, let's review the indications that an adolescent is generally on track in her development. She'll be attending school regularly and will have some concern about at least passing her courses. She'll have a minimum of one or two good friends with whom she'll talk by phone and/or see regularly, as well as having a wider circle of acquaintances with whom she feels comfortable. She'll have some interests, be it sports, an organization, hobbies, musical or artistic pursuits, a job, or being social with friends.

At home she'll have some positive interaction with her parents and siblings, including occasional expressions of affection to them. Although she'll test the house rules once in a while and may complain mightily about things not being fair, she'll basically respect the consequences that are set when she does step out of line. She'll smile and laugh at times, especially when she's inter acting with her friends. And she'll have a normal energy level except for occasions when she has good reason to feel lethargic (up too late, ill).

Now let's contrast this general picture with some specific areas that can constitute a red flag:

DEPRESSION

All adolescents have times when they feel "down" or sad; they might even use the word *depressed* to describe their state of mind, yet may not be talking about what a mental health professional would consider to be an actual depression. When genuine depression is present, the teen often experiences feelings of sadness, even hopelessness and helplessness, that continue over a period of weeks or months. She may lose interest in her normal activities and become more withdrawn. This picture, of course, is similar to what we expect of a depressed adult. However, many depressed teens do *not* show these signs; unlike adults, adolescents will often mask their depression in excessive anger or in rebellious, acting-out behavior.

Now let's look at some specific common indicators that can alert you to the possibility that your teen might be depressed:

- Frequent complaints of sadness, fatigue, and boredom
- Loss of interest or pleasure in usual activities
- Spending *more time than usual* watching television or listening to music
- Oversensitivity, reacting to comments or situations by crying more easily
- Withdrawal or isolation from peers
- Expressing the feeling that "no one likes me" or that friends are "turning on me"
- A low energy level
- A change in sleeping habits, having trouble falling asleep, waking up in the early-morning hours and not being able to go back to sleep, or sleeping too much
- A sudden change in behavior, such as quitting a sports team she's always loved, or a dramatic drop in grades
- Complaints of physical symptoms that have no physical cause
- Verbalizing consistent feelings of guilt, self-blame, or failure
- Beginning to engage in serious acting-out behaviors, such as running away, being sexually promiscuous, abusing alcohol/ drugs, getting involved in gang activity, shoplifting, or engaging in other criminal activity
- School problems, such as frequent tardiness, absenteeism, or skipping classes
- Excessive daydreaming or difficulty concentrating
- Preoccupation with death or suicide, including remarks about being "better off dead"

As you can see, just about any problem a teen can have *might* be an expression of underlying depression. On the other hand, just about any of these potential signs might crop up *occasionally* in a perfectly normal teen; it's their *frequency* and *duration* that make the difference between a red flag and a temporary adolescent crisis.

It's also important to realize that there can be a genuine biological component to teen depression, especially if there has been a history of depression in other family members (grandparents, aunts and uncles, and others). Such chemical problems often begin to emerge after the onset of puberty. When this is the case, antidepressant medication that is prescribed and monitored by a psychiatrist may be necessary (such medication also can be helpful temporarily even if the teen's depression is not thought to be biologically based).

ANGER CONTROL

There's a big difference between a teenager who yells and screams when she's angry and one who loses control and becomes seriously destructive of personal property and/or assaultive to other people. It's one thing to slam a door and maybe throw something unbreakable onto the floor or across the room (in a way that doesn't break or hurt anything or anyone in the vicinity); it's quite another to throw something in a way that causes injury to someone or results in destruction of property. Obviously, grabbing and brandishing any object as a weapon, threatening to injure or kill someone, or launching a physical attack are totally inappropriate methods of expressing anger.

EXCESSIVE REBELLION

Most teens will rebel in some ways. Remember, they have to find something they don't like about their "nest" in order to psychologically gear themselves up to leave it. In fact, adolescents who are highly acquiescent and don't engage in some mildly rebellious behavior (at least occasionally questioning their parents' reasoning and decisions) may be overly dependent and insecure. They are the people who often "do adolescence" in midlife, never having established a firm independent identity of their own.

However, there is such a thing as too much rebellion. Examples include a teen refusing consistently to follow rules about curfews, choosing to stay out all night without permission, basically coming and going as she pleases, refusing any limits or consequences for her actions, and/or consistently carrying on illegal activities or other forbidden behaviors at home. In other words, when rebellion is extreme, a parent has lost all control over the teen's actions.

INAPPROPRIATE SEXUAL BEHAVIOR

Many parents think that a teen's becoming sexually active is always inappropriate. However, from a mental health standpoint, sexual activity per se by an adolescent would not necessarily qualify as a serious problem. The fact is that many perfectly normal teenagers are sexually active, and the degree of "inappropriateness" is dependent on the *circumstances* under which sex occurs.

This whole matter is further complicated by the double standard that exists in our culture: Boys are often expected and/or encouraged to engage in casual sexual encounters without there being any question about the existence of an emotional problem; in contrast, girls who do the same thing are labeled promiscuous and are looked upon as having a personality or emotional problem. Since this is the view of our culture, teenage girls who engage in casual sex on a repeated basis typically *do* have problems with low self-esteem. They *may* also be victims of some form of sexual abuse (earlier molestation, rape, or date rape), and their sexual acting out may represent a form of self-destruction and covert self-blame for feelings of guilt and unworthiness.

ANXIETY AND STRESS

A certain amount of anxiety is productive. However, there is a point at which too much anxiety overloads a person's circuits and creates symptoms of stress, such as chronic worrying, panic attacks, agoraphobia, fearfulness, excessive insecurity, and/or psychosomatic ailments (physical problems for which there is a psychological cause, often called stress-related ailments). The teen who is too much of a perfectionist, whose mind "runs too fast" and creates feelings of exhaustion, whose insecurities hamper normal social interaction, and/or who obsesses about normal daily routine events or duties may be suffering from excessive anxiety.

UNUSUAL EATING HABITS

Many teens eat unhealthily, filling themselves with junk food. While not ideal from a nutritional standpoint, such behavior doesn't signify the presence of an emotional problem. Nor does the typical teen girl who thinks she's a few pounds overweight, or perhaps is overweight, and who sets out to put herself on a diet.

However, the teen who begins severely to limit her eating and is actually thin or who diets to the point of being thin and doesn't *stop* dieting (believing she's still fat) may have an emotional illness called anorexia. Just as serious is the adolescent, overweight or slender, who attempts to control her weight by vomiting or by taking laxatives. A common clue that this may be happening with your teen is if she regularly goes into the bathroom during a meal or within thirty minutes after having finished a meal. This form of eating disorder is called bulimia. Anorexia and bulimia can be present either alone or together. These eating disorders occur much more frequently in females, but occasionally have been reported in males. Both signal the need for professional treatment, as either can lead to serious physical problems, including death.

SUBSTANCE ABUSE AND ADDICTION

The teen who has become addicted to alcohol/drugs, as opposed to the teen who may be using these substances experimentally, requires professional evaluation and treatment. This particular problem was discussed in Chapter Eight.

A MARKED BEHAVIOR CHANGE

Any dramatic *negative change* in an adolescent's pattern of behavior can signal the possibility of a serious underlying emotional problem. This could manifest as a marked increase in mood swings, excessive irritability, unusual eating habits (eating too much or too little food), a noticeable change in sleeping patterns (going without sleep for long periods, or sleeping too much), a sudden drop in school performance, excessive withdrawal from usual interests and activities, sudden secretive behavior, the presence of voices and "visions" that are not apparent to others, or preoccupation with some bizarre interest (witchcraft, Satanism, reading about or experimenting with explosives, etc.).

COMMON DILEMMAS

SUICIDAL THINKING

Seventeen-year-old Stacy has seemed quieter lately. You think she's still upset about her boyfriend's breaking up with her a few weeks earlier, but she insists that she's fine about it. Then you discover her journal, which she's left lying open on the coffee table, and are shocked to read that she's thinking about killing herself.

When you have reason to believe your teen might be thinking about suicide, you'll want to try to draw this information out of her—for example, "Honey, you've seemed so sad lately. I have a strong feeling it's about the breakup," or "I can see how upset you are since your breakup with Stan. Sometimes when people feel this way, they think about trying to hurt themselves, and I don't want you to do this."

In other words, you'll try to get your teen to discuss her suicidal thoughts without admitting you've read her journal, if possible. But if she continues to deny that anything is wrong, you'll need to confront her directly about the journal entry. Especially when a teen has written something private but left it out in plain sight, you can assure her that a part of her wanted help and wanted someone to see the note. On the other hand, if you've deliberately gone through your teen's private things to find this information (which you'd only do if you had *good* reason to suspect that your teen is self-destructive or in some danger), and you cannot get her to admit such thoughts or activities, you'll have to admit that you did violate her privacy and tell her your reasons for having done so.

When your teen does admit that she's been thinking of suicide, keep your conversation with her calm, supportive, and concerned. You want to get information from her in order to assess the potential seriousness of her suicidal thinking. Tell her directly (rather than assuming she knows it) that you would *never* under any circumstances want her to kill herself, no matter what it is she's done or how badly she feels. And, most important, be sure to tell her that you love her and that you will do whatever is in your power to help her.

Sometimes, parents understandably become so distraught about knowing a teen has been having suicidal thoughts that they become angry, saying things like "I can't believe you're even thinking such a ridiculous thing!" Or they might try to minimize the potential seriousness of the situation by accusing the adolescent of "just trying to get attention." Or they might decide simply to ignore the whole matter, chalking up a teen's writing or talking about suicide to "a phase she's going through; almost all teens think about killing themselves at one time or another."

However, *any* time a teen (or child, or adult) talks or writes about the possibility of committing suicide, or the wish to be dead, the statement needs to be assessed and addressed. While it is true that children and teens *can* threaten suicide as an attention-getting tactic, especially when they are angry, or as a way to manipulate a parent, it's just too risky to *assume* that this is the case without pursuing the matter. Even if it is a tactic to get attention, the fact that the teen takes this extreme tack indicates that he or she has serious issues that are crying out to be addressed. Also, teens who don't really want to kill themselves but make a suicide attempt for attention sometimes succeed in actually taking their lives.

Therefore, calmly ask your teen to tell you why she may be thinking of killing herself. If she denies that her suicidal-sounding statements are serious, ask her if she *would* tell you if she *were* serious. Sometimes this will get a reluctant teen to admit that she really is having suicidal thoughts.

Even if she continues to deny that her words are accurate, you'd want to let her know that no matter what type of problem she might be (or was) having, suicide is never a good option. If she's done something she regrets, or if she's feeling hopeless about her life, assure her that you still love her and will get her the help she needs to deal with the situation that's troubling her—no matter what it is.

If your adolescent admits that she is or recently has been thinking of killing herself, ask her how she thinks she would do it. You're asking this question not out of morbid curiosity but to assess the seriousness of her suicidal thoughts. If she tells you that she has no idea, or hasn't really thought about *how* she'd do it, chances are less likely that she is imminently suicidal. Call for an appointment with a mental health professional and continue keeping a close watch on her behavior, activities, and mood. If she does tell you a plan, particularly if it's been well thought out, you would consider her to be a high risk for suicide at that point. *Immediate* consultation with a mental health professional is strongly recommended at that point, and could possibly result in your teen's hospitalization.

If ever you have reason to suspect that your teen (or anyone else) might be suicidal, the best way to find out if this is true is to *ask the person directly.* Many times parents are afraid that asking someone such a question will "put ideas into her head." However, a person who has no intention of killing herself will tell you so, convincingly; she certainly won't run out and make a suicide attempt just because you've asked her about this in a concerned, caring way. A person who is contemplating suicide will usually admit it, often feeling relieved because bringing the matter into the open is the first step in solving the problem.

There are also some indirect signs that a teen might be thinking about suicide, and parents need to be aware of these red flags and not dismiss them as "silly." Teens who begin to write letters to their significant friends and relatives *may* be doing so as a way of saying good-bye. They may also begin to read novels or articles about people who've committed suicide, or to write suicidal poetry. They might begin to give away their important possessions. Certainly, finding out that they've written any form of a will should also be a cause for alarm.

If you see any of these behaviors in your teen, again, ask her directly if she is thinking about killing herself. Also, a *serious* suspicion that your teen might be suicidal is one time most mental health professionals would recommend breaking the boundaries of privacy by searching through your teen's personal possessions, diaries, and so forth.

It never hurts to be aware of those common situations that *might* make it more likely that your teen could contemplate suicide. Examples are the breakup of a significant romantic relationship; failure to achieve some highly anticipated goal, award, or recognition (not being chosen as a cheerleader, not getting into the desired college, not getting a sought-after scholarship, being kicked off a sports team, etc.); the death of a parent, friend, or any highly valued person (especially if that person committed suicide); the presence of a life-threatening illness in a teen; or some humiliating experience (being caught cheating, being raped, being publicly ridiculed, or having one's family ridiculed) in the newspaper or other media.

If you think your teen could be, is, or recently has been suicidal, it's wise to take necessary precautions at home as well as getting her professional help. If you (or your teen) own a gun, lock it up, and lock up ammunition for it in a separate place. Look through your medicine cabinets, removing dangerous amounts of prescription or nonprescription drugs and locking them up. You can leave small amounts of nonprescription items there, but nothing that, taken in its entirety, would cause serious physical repercussions. If you're not sure, ask your family physician or call a poison control center.

RAGE

Fifteen-year-old Boyce has always had a temper, but he's becoming more explosive. One evening, infuriated with you for insisting that he clean his room, he smashes a hole in the wall with his fist.

If you witness your teen becoming rageful and destructive, tell him firmly, but without high emotion, to calm himself down. If he's done something physically destructive, check him to see if he's injured, and give him appropriate treatment, if necessary. In the heat of the crisis, do not try to talk with him about his behavior, make negative comments about his immaturity, lecture him about the terrible things that "could have happened," or discuss the particulars of how he will have to repair and/or pay for any property damage. Give him some space by allowing him to go to his room or some other place where he feels comfortable, letting him know that the two of you will discuss the situation later, after he's cooled off.

If you discover, after the fact, that your teen has destroyed property, tell him at the first opportunity that you want to talk about what happened ("How come that hole is in your wall?"). When discussing the incident, whether you witnessed it earlier or just discovered it, try to convey curiosity rather than contempt. You want to be clear that you consider his behavior to be inappropriate, but in a concerned way that implies that you know he probably feels bad about it too. You'll want to find out what made him so frustrated or angry, and to determine, if possible, if there was some circumstance that caused him to lose control (using drugs, not sleeping for several nights, or other stresses).

You'll also want to problem-solve with your teen about ways that he can release such feelings in the future in an *appropriate* manner. Helpful forms of anger management include performing some physical activity (jogging, lifting weights, mowing the lawn, cleaning the bathroom, or performing push-ups or sit-ups), calling a friend to vent the anger to a sympathetic ear, listening to soothing music and/or lying down to relax, writing an uncensored version of the angry feelings in a journal, or hitting or pounding on something that is appropriate for this purpose (a mattress, a pillow, a tackling dummy hung from the ceiling in a garage or utility room, or a punching bag).

Encourage your teen to commit to experimenting with one or more of these techniques the next time he feels frustrated or angry. Also, warn him about the need to vent anger or frustration when he first becomes aware of it rather than letting such feelings build to the point of explosive rage.

Once you've talked things out, ask your teen how he can be responsible for correcting any damage he's done, either by repairing it or by paying for a replacement. Depending on the extent of the damage and the circumstances surrounding the incident, you might also want to set an additional negative consequence (removal of one or more of his privileges) until he repairs or repays the damage.

Certainly, if your teen continues with his rageful or destructive behavior, or if he's threatened to (or has) physically hurt someone, consultation with a mental health professional is recommended.

CRIMINAL BEHAVIOR

You answer your doorbell at two A.M. to find your fourteen-year-old son, Ned, accompanied by a policeman. The officer informs you that your son has been caught stealing stereos and radar detectors from cars.

One of the hardest times for a parent to allow the natural consequences of a teen's actions to occur is when legal issues are involved. No parents want their teenager to have an arrest record; consequently, some will go to great lengths (and expense) to manipulate the legal system in order to get their teen's charges dismissed.

For most first offenses, however, the laws usually provide a way for a teenager to fulfill his penalty via some type of probation, fine, and/or community service. In addition, adolescents are often required to participate in an educational course related to shoplifting, theft, DWI charges, and other legal infractions. Even if a teen has to go to some type of "boot camp" via the judicial system, all infractions while he's a minor can often be erased from his file when he legally becomes an adult.

Difficult as it may be, it's generally best to allow a teen to follow through with whatever legal measures are prescribed by the juvenile court. This provides a far better opportunity for him to learn a genuine lesson from his actions than all the talking to, reasoning, and grounding that a parent can dish out. Of course, parents often have strong resentment about the financial and emotional costs that go along with legal proceedings. Know that it's very normal for parents to struggle with tremendous anger toward a teen who has created such distress.

In addition to whatever legal consequences occur, it is also wise to consult a mental health professional to determine what is behind your teen's illegal behavior. Is he rebelling because of a family problem? Is he caving in to pressure, perhaps even from a gang, in order to fit in with a particular group of peers? Is he making a bid for attention? Does his behavior represent a cry for help due to an underlying depression? Does he have deeper character problems that need to be addressed?

But what happens if it is the *parent* who discovers that a teenager is breaking the law, rather than the police or some other authority outside the family? What if *you* open your son's closet and find stolen merchandise? Or find out that your daughter has hidden a shoplifted item in her wardrobe?

Whether or not you report your teen to the proper authorities will depend on the extent of the crime. If you were to discover a large volume of stolen items, it would be best to report your teen. On the other hand, if it is a few items, which can be returned to stores or owners, you could insist that your adolescent return the items *in person* to the owners and/or make appropriate restitution (e.g., paying for stolen clothes that have already been worn).

In such a case, you would also want to set consequences at home for your teen's behavior. Whether or not you consult a mental health professional at that point is a judgment call. Some teens will shoplift in the same experimental sense that they will sneak out at night. If you believe that this is a first occurrence for your teen, that he is truly remorseful, and you don't think he's having significant family or emotional problems, you could see how things go without professional intervention. Obviously, you'd want to be alert to any recurrence of the same behavior, and definitely seek professional help if, in fact, it develops.

Realize that it's very easy for a parent to deny that a teen is stealing. It's only human to tend to perceive (or misperceive) events that support our beliefs and to ignore or rationalize things that might threaten to bring out some unpleasant or frightening truth that we really don't want to face. Consequently, we may not question our adolescents about items we see them wearing or using, or we may too easily buy into the "I borrowed it from a friend" alibi.

The fact remains that there are informal ways of checking these things out without seeming unduly suspicious. For example, when one of your teen's friends (from whom she says she "borrowed" a sweater) is visiting, you might take the opportunity when your teen is out of the room to ask her where she purchased that terrific green-and-white-striped sweater. If she denies owning one, you have your answer.

Certainly, if your teen has been caught stealing, it would be appropriate to make a "no borrowing from friends" rule, unless there's been prior parental consent. If your teen accuses you of mistrust, admit that you have reason not to trust her in this area and that it is now *her* responsibility to prove that she has become trustworthy. After several months have passed without a similar incident, you can let her know that you are now ready to trust her again and that she can resume borrowing clothes from her friends.

RUNNING AWAY

After an argument with you earlier in the day, seventeen-year-old Marci stormed to her room in a huff. You went to the supermarket to give her time to cool off, and returned to find a note on the kitchen counter saying that she has run away from home. When you check her room, you see that most of her clothes, jewelry, and makeup are gone and that she's taken the money she'd been saving for a CD player out of her desk drawer.

Most parents are filled with disbelief, fury, fear, and/or sadness when they face this situation. Some get in the car immediately and begin driving around trying to locate their teen; others begin calling all of her friends or the places where they think she might have gone. Some call the police to report the teen as a runaway, only to find that a person must be missing for twenty-four hours before the police will take any action.

If parents are unsuccessful in finding a teen, they face the most difficult thing of all: waiting to hear from her. Generally, the later it gets at night, the higher the parent's anxiety will rise.

Many times, the call comes, often with the teen saying that she's not revealing her location but wants you to know she's okay. Although parents typically feel somewhat relieved, they're likely to remain scared and upset to realize that they are relatively helpless in this situation.

At this point, most parents ask the teen to return home; unfortunately, the request is often turned down. If this happens, it's probably best to reassure your adolescent that no matter how angry the two of you might be (or have been) with each other, you don't want her to leave home. Suggest that she tell you where she is (to set your mind at ease so that you can get some sleep) but that you will not come to get her. Let her know that so long as she's in a safe place, you will let her stay there overnight, but that you'd like her to come home at a designated time tomorrow and calmly discuss whatever is the matter.

If she refuses to tell you where she is, try to get her to agree to a specific time when she will come home, or to a place where the two of you can meet the next day. If she says she needs a couple of days, it's probably best to go along with this request and give her some space. If school is in session, encourage her to continue going to school and reassure her that you will give her the time she needs to think things over. If worse comes to worst, and she refuses to tell you where she is or to agree on a specific time to meet, ask her to call you the next evening after she's had some time to think.

In other words, try to get as much of a commitment as you can, but don't push an issue and alienate her further. Your goal at this stage is simply to get her back home, or at least to meet with you to talk things out.

Whenever this meeting occurs, ask your teenager to tell you why she felt she had to leave home. Refrain from jumping in with your own analysis of the situation before you've heard her story, and just *listen*. Hopefully, your discussion will allow the two of you to air your differences and negotiate a way of resolving them.

If the two of you are not able to problem-solve a possible solution to the dispute, consult a mental health professional for objective advice. In fact, an agreement that your teen will see a therapist, either individually or in family therapy, might be a part of a contract drawn up between you. If she refuses, it can still be very useful for you and your mate to consult a therapist in order to help you deal with the issues presented by your adolescent.

If the meeting with your teen does not alleviate some of the tension between you, consider allowing her to stay with a relative or friend for a brief time or, if there is a lot of hostility, for a longer period. It may be that you can convince her to go to family therapy by making this concession.

But what if you are faced with your teenager *threatening* to run away? Often, parents are so angry in such a situation that they say things they don't mean, such as "Well, go ahead! I couldn't care less!" or "Great! I'll help you pack!" Since it's very unlikely that you really would want your teen to run away, it's best not to fuel her rebellious flames. Tell her the truth: No matter how angry you or she become with each other, your home is her home, and you continue to love her even when you are angry with her. The way to solve a family problem is to face it, getting professional help if necessary, rather than to run from it.

EATING DISORDERS

Fifteen-year-old Lauri began a strict diet about three months ago. Now she's lost twenty pounds and is looking extremely thin, yet she continues to see herself as fat. You're alarmed because she is preoccupied with calories and restricts herself to very little food.

When a teen is losing too much weight, you will want to have her evaluated immediately by a physician. If a physical cause is ruled out, she may be diagnosed as having anorexia. This emotionally based disorder results from a teen's literally starving herself while believing, against all reality, that she is overweight.

Typically, she has such a distorted body image that all attempts to reason with her about her actual size fall on deaf ears; she simply denies the reality that's so obvious to everyone else. Often, she'll engage in obsessive thinking about food, severely limiting her food choices to items such as salad or broth, all the while maintaining that she is not at all hungry.

Anorexia requires both physical and psychological intervention, since too much weight loss can severely compromise health and can even result in death. Due to the seriousness of the disorder, physicians will hospitalize an anorexic patient if their body weight falls to an extreme degree, using intravenous feedings to create weight gain. This is why a teen's physical status should always be monitored by a physician *in addition to* her being treated for the psychological issues that give rise to the problem.

A related eating disorder is bulimia, the name given to a cycle of binging on food and then purging oneself (by vomiting and/or by taking laxatives). The bulimic teenager may be overweight, or she may also be anorexic. As mentioned earlier, parents can be alerted to this behavior when a teen consistently leaves the table during meals, or goes into the bathroom within thirty minutes of eating. Later stages of this disorder will produce a soft, silky hair on the arms and face, as well as a loss of enamel from the teeth. Bulimia can easily become an addictive behavior and is also severely dangerous to health.

Both anorexia and bulimia are found more commonly in females, but also occur in males. The psychological dynamics of these disorders can be very complicated. They require treatment by a mental health professional with experience in treating eating disorders. Psychotherapy is often combined with input from a nutritionist or dietitian, as well as the monitoring of the teen's weight gain (or loss) by a physician.

If your teen is involved in dance, gymnastics, cheerleading, modeling, or other pursuits where a slim body specifically is desired, you'll want to be especially alert to the possibility of her developing anorexia in a quest for a lean body. All teenagers, however, need to be warned about the physical dangers of trying to be too thin. Professional consultation is recommended if there is any suspicion that an adolescent may be developing anorexia or bulimia, before it becomes a serious medical condition.

GANG ACTIVITY

You're reading a newspaper article about items of clothing that symbolize involvement in a local gang. Suddenly, it dawns on you that fourteen-year-old Larry has been wearing some of these exact items.

Parents often naively think that gangs exist only in "other" neighborhoods than their own. The fact is that gangs exist in neighborhoods from the most affluent to the poorest, making it important for all parents to be on the alert for possible signs that their adolescent might be becoming involved in gang activity.

Certainly, if your teen begins to dress in some unusual way, it is wise to check with the school counselor or principal to make sure that the attire doesn't indicate gang membership. However, there are other possible warning signs, besides his clothing, that your teen might be in a gang.

One of the best indicators is the appearance of graffiti on your teen's backpack, book jackets, and notebooks (see the insides too). All gangs have special symbols and/or a code language, which they use to communicate both with their own members as well as with other gangs.

Another common sign is that your teen suddenly has a new nickname. If the name seems ominous in some way, if it is a word that you don't recognize, or if you don't readily understand why your teen is pegged with that particular name, again, check it out by talking to school personnel.

Obviously, sometimes the first sign that your teen may be interested in or getting involved in a gang is that he begins to hang out with a new peer group of "troublemakers." If his friends are involved in delinquent acts, skip out of school often, are frequently in physical fights, or are known to be in a gang, there is a good possibility that your teen *may* be involved in the same activities.

It is important to realize that many teens who do show some of these signs may not yet have joined a gang, but are flirting with the possibility. This is why it is so important to pick up on these gang signs as quickly as possible, in hopes of preventing your teen from formal initiation. Once a teen becomes a true gang member, it may be extremely difficult to get him out of it without some harm coming to him or to another family member.

If you are certain that your teen is hanging out with known gang members, this is one time to step in and forbid the association. If he has already joined a gang, the best solution may be to move your teen out of town in order to protect him. If this is not possible, find out if your community has a shelter for teens who are leaving gangs (much like battered women's shelters). If your teen insists that he does not want to get out of a gang, see the following section ("Out of Control").

If none of these solutions is available, there is one other option. Gather a large group of adults (six to ten) made up of several family members (including uncles, cousins, and other relatives) *as well as* a few nonfamily members (a minister, community leader, and/or friends of the family). Have the *entire group* go together to visit your teen's best gang friends at their individual homes, preferably with their parents present. Tell each one that your teen is leaving the gang and that if any harm comes to him or to any member of his family, the group will hold *that* teen personally responsible. Gang members often don't even discuss these visits with one another, not wanting to appear intimidated, but will influence their gang to leave the exiting teen alone. By involving adults who are not family members, the power of the group is magnified tremendously.

You may also be able to move your teen to another school, even within the same public school district, if the new school's administration is aware that your teen is leaving a gang. Obviously, you would also want your teen to consult with a mental health professional to determine the root of your teen's wish to belong to a gang. Family therapy might be in order to correct problems at home that may be exacerbating the situation. Even if your teen leaves town, psychotherapy in the new location would be highly recommended.

Many teens who want to or who do join a gang have problems with self-esteem. Their rebellious stance often conceals an underlying depression. They feel misunderstood, unsupported, or alienated; gang membership offers them a feeling of instant belonging to a group who demands nothing more of them than surrender to the gang's control. As long as the teen does what is required by the gang leaders, he is praised for his loyalty and held in high esteem by the members.

As a preventive measure, get your teen involved in *positive* groups. It is not inappropriate to make his privileges contingent on his pursuing some constructive interest, be it playing a sport, participating in a school or church organization, or involving himself in some other activity (working out in a health club, spending time developing a hobby). If he flatly refuses to do any of these and is old enough to work, insist that he get a job. If he's too young to be employed and can't seem to find any extracurricular interest, give him the option of doing volunteer work or community service. The point is that kids who are kept busy with constructive activities do not usually become involved in gangs.

OUT OF CONTROL

Seventeen-year-old Hal refuses to accept any rules and does exactly what he pleases. You feel totally frustrated and powerless.

Some adolescents, especially those in their late teens, get to a point where they refuse to accept any parental authority. They refuse to do household chores. They allow their friends to come over and mess up the house and never clean up after themselves. They flagrantly disregard "no smoking" or "no drinking" rules and refuse to accept a curfew. Sometimes they stay out all night, not bothering to let parents know where they are or that they're not planning to come home.

Some teens who are out of parental control will pay lip service to changing their behavior, yet never follow through with their promises. Most, however, are overtly rebellious. They become easily angered when parents try to talk to them about their lack of consideration and responsibility, often walking out of the room or leaving the house when they are confronted.

Usually, this dismal situation occurs when parents allow a young adolescent to have too much freedom too soon. It can be extremely difficult, if not impossible, to regain parental control once it is lost, especially once the teen becomes an older adolescent. This is why it's a good preventive measure to seek consultation with a mental health professional if you notice that your young adolescent is vehemently testing or flouting the rules. You'll need to nip such behavior in the bud and regain control *before* your teen is legally of age to work, to drive, to drop out of school, or to refuse inpatient psychiatric or chemical dependency treatment (if needed). You'll also need to regain control while you still have some leverage; most younger teens are still dependent on their parents to provide spending money, a phone, a car to drive, and other creature comforts.

It's also important to be aware of the discrepancy between the way families, schools, and the law determine when a teen is "of legal age." For example, parents are often shocked when they discover that a teen can legally drop out of school at age sixteen or seventeen, even without parental consent. Or, in a case where the family of a cocaine-addicted seventeen-year-old seeks to have the teen admitted to a psychiatric facility for treatment, parents are dismayed to learn that there's nothing a parent can do to get the teen admitted *without the teen's consent*, since he's seventeen. These facts highlight the need for parents to seek professional help when problems first appear in early adolescence.

Using behavior contracts and working on family issues in psychotherapy can often repair family problems and bring a teen back into appropriate parental control. Parents can be taught to set reasonable and effective limits on their teens, and both generations can learn communication skills that will improve their relationship.

Unfortunately, sometimes parents will try to regain control when it's too late. The teen knows that a parent's discipline is impotent; consequently, he ignores it. Some teens will refuse to participate in any type of counseling or therapy, and the parent has no leverage to get him to change his mind. When this happens, it is still helpful for parents to get professional help for *themselves* regarding what might be done to assist their teen and/or family.

If this situation occurs with your teen *after you've tried* contracts and psychotherapy (if you could get your teen to attend), you'll have to make a difficult decision: either to allow him to remain at home or to ask (or insist) that he leave. Factors that might lead to the latter decision include your teen's engaging in harmful and/or illegal activities in your home (dealing drugs out of your house; throwing drinking/drugging parties when you're not at home), seriously influencing younger children in a negative way (actively encouraging them to rebel against you; engaging in blatant sexual behavior around younger siblings), or having poor emotional control (becoming violent, destroying property).

Of course, even if he isn't doing any of these things, you still have to consider your own personal well-being. Is your teen's remaining at home creating emotional problems for you? Is your marriage in serious danger of breaking up because of the intense conflict? Is your physical health being compromised?

On the other hand, it might be that even though you don't like your teen's behavior, you are able to remain somewhat detached from it. If he's not endangering you or the family physically or legally, and if he's not continually filling the house with hostility, you may prefer to allow him to continue to live at home until he graduates from high school.

If you do decide that he needs to leave the house, be prepared for the likely possibility that he might want to return in a few weeks or months. If you allow him to come home, be sure that you and he establish the house rules *beforehand* (as well as the behaviors that would result in his being asked to leave the house again) and that you have good reason to believe that he's changed his attitude and/or his behavior. Resist the temptation to allow him to come home *only* because he's gotten into more trouble or has run out of options, rather than because he has made a gain in maturity. If this is difficult for you, consider joining a parent support group such as Tough Love (see discussion at end of Chapter Eight).

SOME FINAL THOUGHTS

Now that you've reviewed some typical and not-so-typical teen issues, you may be feeling a bit overwhelmed! So let's pull together a few basic principles of relating to your teenager that you've read about in these pages, just to remind you of how much you already know:

- Listen *before* you express your views
- Refrain from lectures, exhortations, and hysterics
- Be clear about what you are asking your teen to do
- Teach responsibility by relating actions to consequences
- Link increased privileges with *demonstrated* responsibility
- Don't get your feelings hurt when your teen prefers being with friends to being with you
- Show respect for your teen's views, even if you disagree with them
- Let yourself be interrupted when your teen is ready to talk
- Don't lose your sense of humor
- Be a parent, not a "best friend"
- With any given incident, realize that it will probably seem insignificant when your teen is thirty
- Be gentle with yourself

Above all, remember that those adolescent years contain many wonderful moments for teen and parent alike. Be free with your encouragement, patience, affection, and unconditional love.

I NDEX